WITHOUT THORNS, IT'S NOT A ROSE

Fr. John M. Scott, S.J.

Our Sunday Visitor Publishing Division
Our Sunday Visitor, Inc.
Huntington, Indiana 46750

International Standard Book Number: 0-87973-502-3
Library of Congress Catalog Card Number: 86-62479

Cover design by James E. McIlrath

PRINTED IN THE UNITED STATES OF AMERICA

502

Acknowledgments

Scripture texts appearing in this book are taken from the *Revised Standard Version Bible, Catholic Edition,* © 1965 and 1966 by the Division of Christian Education of the National Council of the Churches of Christ in the U.S.A., and used by permission of the copyright owner; also the *New American Bible,* © 1970 by the Confraternity of Christian Doctrine, Washington, D.C., and are used by license of said copyright owner. Among other sources from which material has been excerpted or has served as the basis for portions of this book, and for which the author is grateful, are: in Chapter 1, the Ann Landers letter published by newspapers subscribing to the Field Newspaper Syndicate (permission to use this material granted by Ann Landers and the Field Newspaper Syndicate); in Chapter 2, excerpts from "The Convergence of Science and Religion," which appeared in the March-April 1966 edition of *Think* magazine (permission granted by the author); in Chapter 3, excerpts from *Fully Human, Fully Alive,* by Rev. John Powell, S.J., © 1976 by Argus Communications, Allen, Texas; in Chapter 4, Milton's "Paradise Lost" and other poetry reprinted from the *Loyola Book of Verse,* © 1933 by Loyola University Press, Chicago; in Chapter 6, material reprinted by permission of *Guideposts* Magazine, © 1976 by Guideposts Associates, Inc., Carmel, N.Y.; also in Chapter 6, "My God Is No Stranger," by Helen Steiner Rice, reprinted by permission of the author and Gibson Greeting Cards, Inc.; special thanks go to *Reader's Digest* for material in Chapter 7 excerpted from "You Can't Quit," by Hubert H. Humphrey, appearing in the August 1977 issue of *Reader's Digest;* the author also thanks *Sunshine Magazine* for the poem by Everett Wentworth Hill, also in Chapter 7; Mr. H.V. Morton, for excerpts from his book, *A Traveller in Rome,* published by Dodd, Mead, and Co., New York, which appear in Chapter 9; Random House, New York, for excerpts from *Anne Frank: Diary of a Young Girl,* which appear in Chapter 5; *Catholic Digest* magazine, for excerpts from "Clare Boothe Luce Looks Ahead" (May 1979 edition), which appear in Chapter 6; and to the many other kind and generous individuals and publishers who have made this book a reality. If any copyrighted materials have been inadvertently used in this book without proper credit being given, please notify Our Sunday Visitor in writing so that future printings of this work may be corrected accordingly.

*Dedicated to
my mother and father
whose acceptance
of life's crosses
was an inspiration
to all who knew them*

Contents

Introduction • 7

1 • Screaming at God • 9

2 • A Nobel Prize Winner to the Rescue • 23

3 • Why Job Stopped Screaming • 43

4 • From Blind Milton to the Jungle Doctor • 57

5 • From the Trenches of World War I to Vietnam • 67

6 • Gallant Women • 85

7 • Stouthearted Men • 108

8 • The Magic of Enthusiasm • 132

9 • New Horizons • 148

10 • Adventures Unlimited • 166

Introduction

This book is unique in that it approaches the problem of suffering in much the same way that God did when he responded to Job's lamentations and objections.

When Job complained about his many sufferings and woes, God answered him by using a fascinating "scientific method." This same "scientific method" we may use today to acquire a new outlook on the problem of suffering.

Nobel Prize winner Dr. Charles H. Townes alerts us to the fact that too often we act as though the mystery of suffering is the only unknown in our lives. The dazzling truth is that we are completely surrounded by mysteries on all sides. If only we become aware of this fact, then the mystery of suffering will take its rightful place as a part of the mysterious universe, which we do not understand.

"Paradoxes do not destroy our faith," says Dr. Townes. "They simply remind us of a limited understanding."

The best "sermons" urging us to apply the

"scientific method" in our own lives can be found in the inspiring lives of great men and women throughout history. It has been said that "one does not have to occupy a pulpit to preach a powerful sermon. That of living so as to bless and inspire others does more." Chapters 4 to 7 of this book include many such inspiring "sermons."

Chapter 9 takes us far beyond the "scientific method." It fascinates us with the thrilling news about the "rediscovery" of the joy of Christianity and the true meaning of Easter. We can accept the sufferings of this life in patience if we learn and teach a genuinely resurrection-centered theology. The resurrection of our Lord should be a brilliant sun that lights our whole existence every day of our lives.

JOHN M. SCOTT, S.J.

CHAPTER ONE

Screaming at God

**How many times in your life have you
been so mad at God for the way he
was "mistreating" you that you felt**
an urge to scream out in anger?

If you feel like blowing your stack and
telling God off now and then because of his
"failure" to run the world in proper fashion,
then welcome to the "Screamers Club."

According to Father Arthur McNally, C.P.,
it is hard to read the book of Job without coming
to the conclusion that Job was one of the most
impatient people in the Bible. "Much of the time
he doesn't talk to God — he screams at God."

We can imagine Job shouting at God:
"Therefore I will not restrain my mouth; / I will
speak in the anguish of my spirit; / I will
complain in the bitterness of my soul" (Job
7:11).

Job continues his lamentation by saying: "I
will say to God: Do not put me in the wrong! /
Let me know why you oppose me. / Is it a
pleasure for you to oppress, / to spurn the work

of your hands, . . . / Even though you know that I am not wicked. . . ?" (Job 10:2-3, 7).

Job's anguish is so great that he asks: "Why did I not perish at birth, / come forth from the womb and expire? / . . . I should prefer choking / and death rather than my pains" (Job 3:11; 7:15).

Job was a pious and upright man who suffered a sudden and complete reversal of fortune. God took away from Job everything that was precious to him. A loathsome disease afflicted his body. Worst of all, Job is given no explanation of why his life is suddenly tipped upside down.

No wonder Job screams: "I will give free utterance to my complaint; . . . / I was at ease, and he [God] broke me asunder; / he seized me by the neck and dashed me to pieces; / he set me up as his target, / his archers surround me. / He slashes open my kidneys, and does not spare; / he pours out my gall on the ground. / . . . he runs upon me like a warrior" (Job 10:1; 16:12-14).

In frustration and agony Job asks: "Has not man a hard service upon earth, / and are not his days like the days of a hireling? / . . . I am allotted months of emptiness, / and nights of misery are apportioned to me" (Job 7:1, 3).

Job is enraged by what is happening, and when his friends try to counsel him to accept it all without protest, this makes him even more furious.

Job, however, is not the only person in the Old Testament who was exasperated by the way God treated him. In the book of Numbers we read that Moses was so irritated he said to God — actually he probably ranted and raved: "If this is the way you will deal with me, then please do me the favor of killing me at once, so that I need no longer face this distress" (Numbers 11:15).

To cite another example, we find in the first book of Kings that Elijah "went a day's journey into the wilderness, and came and sat down under a broom tree; and he asked that he might die, saying, 'It is enough; now, O Lord, take away my life;'. . ." (1 Kings 19:4).

The prophet Jeremiah also felt that God had mistreated him. Forced to endure many trials and sufferings, he was so drained emotionally that he had grave doubts whether God's promised help would ever come. Vexed by several years of unfulfilled prophecy, Jeremiah accused God of being unfaithful to his word. Jeremiah told God in no uncertain terms: "You duped me, O Lord, and I let myself be duped; / you were too strong for me, and you triumphed. / . . . Whenever I speak, I must cry out, / violence and outrage is my message; . . ." (Jeremiah 20:7-8).

Jeremiah cannot understand why God

seems to have been playing him for a fool, and asks: / "Tell me, LORD, have I not served you for their good? / . . . You know I have. / Why is my pain continuous, / my wound incurable, refusing to be healed? / You have indeed become for me a treacherous brook, / whose waters do not abide!" (Jeremiah 15:11, 18).

Being mad at God seems almost like an occupational hazard for many of the prophets of the Old Testament. In the book of Jonah we read that events became "greatly displeasing to Jonah, and he became angry" (Jonah 4:1).

Jonah was so angry and upset with God that he blurted out: " 'And now, LORD, please take my life from me; for it is better for me to die than to live.' But the LORD asked, 'Have you reason to be angry?' . . . 'I have reason to be angry,' Jonah answered, 'angry enough to die' " (Jonah 4:3-4, 9).

Down through the centuries people in various walks of life have continued to express their feelings as did the prophets of old. They did not suppress anger and disappointment. They knew that God was big enough to take our anger, loving enough to listen to our doubts. Their reward for such honesty was a deeper relationship with their Creator.

The story is told that when St. Theresa of Ávila was on a trip, she fell off her donkey and landed in a mud puddle. As she sank into the thick ooze, her anger leaped upward like a rocket. Looking up into the heavens she shouted, "If this is the way you treat your friends, God, no wonder you have so few of them."

Writing in the *St. Anthony Messenger* for June 1982, Anthony E. Gilles continues with the reaction of the prophets of old: "Lord, things aren't going too well, and you just don't seem to care. I get so angry at you. Are you God, or aren't you?

"Lord, I feel like a real mess. How come you let me be the way I am? I'm mad at you, Lord. That situation at work is terrible, and you won't do anything about it. Will you, *please*, do something about it?"

In the *Catholic Digest* for August 1982, Mrs. Jean Jones informs us that following the death of her husband, she was overcome with long weeks of shock and grief. "Suddenly, on the way to work one day, I shouted out in the car, 'Where are you, God?' I felt he had deserted me when I needed him the most."

The first time I felt like blowing my stack at God was in the summer of 1948 when I was appointed chaplain at St. John's Hospital in St. Louis. As I stood by the bedside of a dying girl in her hospital room I felt as though a giant python had snaked its coils around my chest and was squeezing the air from my lungs. A sensation of utter helplessness clamped me tight like the steel jaws of a vise. I looked down into the pain-filled eyes of the dying girl. I shuddered to see how her delicate little body was jerked and pulled by wires of pain. The girl's parents sat by the side of her bed. Their faces were drained of all hope.

The courageous young girl tried to stifle her cries of pain. Slowly she stretched out her weak fingers and grasped her father's hand. The scene of terrible suffering and utter hopelessness was too much for me. I felt as though a time bomb were ticking inside me. A surge of anger raced up my throat as my lips formed an unspoken question, "Oh, God! Don't you see what is taking place? Why do you allow this innocent child to suffer such agony?"

During the many years that have followed the summer of 1948, I have been chaplain in various hospitals and nursing homes. The one question that patients ask me most often is, "Why can't I die? Why do I have to endure these long days of pain and confinement? I wish that God would take me home today."

The poet María Christina A. Sánchez informs us, "I fear not death but the pain of life." When some people meet pain and suffering they do more than get mad at God: They deny his existence.

During the spring and summer of 1982, a play called "Sister Mary Ignatius Explains It All for You" was offered at the Wisdom Bridge Theater in Chicago. Four of Sister Ignatius' former students have returned to embarrass the nun, whom for different reasons they all hate. The anchor of the four is a woman we will call Diane, a woman who has had two abortions.

Diane is especially angry because she says she believed what the nun had taught about living a good life. Her mother died a long, painful death from cancer.

Diane's prayers for her mother to be cured or to die swiftly were not answered. Sister Mary Ignatius claimed that God had answered "No" to the prayers, but Diane concluded that God was either malicious because he chose to let a good woman suffer, that God was useless because he could not stop her mother's suffering, or that God was nonexistent because he never heard the prayers.

Let us ponder Diane's situation as we read the following poignant lines penned by an unknown poet:

> Some men say there is a God
> And others say no God exists
> Because, they think, an all-wise Creator
> Would not have made a world like this
> Where children starve or die in pain,
> Where want and hunger, war, disease,
> Not to mention work and death,
> Make the place a real valley of tears.

Some people take still another view of suffering. I have on my desk a letter from a woman who writes: "My girl friend was saying that God being good never wishes illness or catastrophes on us. We get them because of something terrible we have done. What do you think?"

It's an age-old question: Why does a merciful and loving God allow suffering and violence in the world?

Father Carroll Stuhlmueller, a Passionist priest, is professor of Old Testament studies at the Catholic Theological Union, Chicago. He received his doctorate at the Pontifical Biblical Institute in Rome. He has been president of the Catholic Biblical Association. According to Father Stuhlmueller, the Bible does not give us a final answer on dealing with suffering.

Father John L. McKenzie is rated as one of the top biblical scholars in the world. Father McKenzie informs us that nowhere in the Bible is there any indication of why we suffer. No one, not even Christ himself, gave an answer. Instead, our Lord showed us a way to live with it by telling us: "Father, . . . not my will but yours be done" (Luke 22:42).

At a memorial Mass for several Creighton University students who were killed in an accident during the winter of 1981, Father Richard Hauser, S.J., said, "Nowhere in the Gospels is there even a hint why God allows us to suffer. God does not send us pain. He allows it to happen — for some unknown reason. God loves us. Our dear departed ones now dwell in love with Christ. We shall all one day be together in a family reunion of joy. The knowledge of all this gives us the strength to endure."

On July 27, 1977, in Prospect, Connecticut, funeral services were held for eight victims of the worst mass murder in the state's history — a young mother and her seven children. Thirty-four pallbearers carried the caskets to the Prospect town cemetery just across the road from the church — six pallbearers for twenty-nine-year-old Cheryl Beaudoin and four for each of her children.

"How could something like this happen?" This was the question that Father Joseph Donnelly asked friends and relatives who crowded St. Anthony of Padua Church, which has a seating capacity of eight hundred fifty.

"Why does God let this go on?" continued Father Donnelly. "Why do the innocent suffer? And yet, as surely as we have all asked these questions, we have all found that there are no answers — none at all."

On Sunday, October 30, 1977, I had the good luck to attend an inspiring adult-education class at St. Gabriel's Parish in Prairie du Chien, Wisconsin. The speaker was Father John Heagle, a gifted theology teacher.

"Christianity does *not* have the answer for suffering," said Father Heagle. "Christianity is an invitation to 'let go and enter into life.' Look where Christianity can take us — to our *resurrection!*"

Father Heagle continued: "Christianity gives us a window on eternity. The 'Good News' of the Gospel is that life is a gift of unfolding love that will blossom into our resurrection. Christianity is a most enriching, mind-expanding way of life."

When I was a young boy growing up in the Copper City of Butte, Montana, I used to watch my mother make rugs from old rags. I was always amazed to see that from the bottom side the rug appeared to be a mad jumble of odds and ends without any plan whatsoever. But when the rug was finished, and viewed from the top side, it contained a delightful, pleasing pattern.

No wonder the poet-priest Father John B. Tabb wrote:

> My life is but a weaving
> Between my God and me;
> I may not choose the colors,
> He knows what they should be;
> For He can view the pattern
> Upon the upper side
> While I can see it only
> On this, the under side.
>
> Sometimes He weaveth sorrow
> Which seemeth strange to me,
> But I will trust His judgment
> And work on faithfully.

'Tis He who fills the shuttle
He knows just what is best
So I shall weave in earnest
And leave with Him the rest.

At last, when life is ended
With Him I shall abide,
Then I may view the pattern
Upon the upper side,
Then I shall know the reason
Why pain with joy entwined
Was woven in the fabric
Of life that God designed.

To me, the most inspiring radio talk given by Pope Pius XII was the one he made from his bed of suffering, shortly before his death. The Holy Father wanted to give a radio talk to comfort those who, like himself, were very ill and confined to a bed of pain. In his talk he particularly spoke to young people who, in their sense of the injustice of their ills, ask, "Why should a good God condemn me to suffer?"

The pope pointed out to his radio audience that God permitted his Son to suffer on the cross, yet what evil had Jesus done? Referring to our Blessed Mother, Pope Pius said, "She did not curse. She did not ask God why. She and her Son suffered voluntarily in full conformity with the divine design. So learn to utter 'so be it' in resignation and patience." The pope was so weak that in the middle of a sentence his voice failed, and one of the attending priests had to continue reading the script.

The question "What have I done to deserve all this trouble?" prompted the following letter to Ann Landers:

> Dear Ann: I am a registered nurse who has worked hard all my life. My husband ran off 10 years ago and I have tried to raise three daughters by myself.
>
> Sixteen months ago, the eldest divorced her husband because he molested one of their little girls. Three months later, the youngest (age 17) turned up pregnant and had an abortion. It later came out that she was entertaining her boyfriend while I worked the night shift. Last week my middle daughter told me she is in love with a married man.
>
> I realize all this sounds like a soap opera, but I swear every word of it is true. What have I done to deserve all this trouble? Please print an answer. I am ashamed to sign my name or give an address. [It was signed, "Heartsick Mother."]
>
> Dear Mother: First, get over the idea that people who have trouble

> "deserve" it. Nothing could be further
> from the truth.
>
> No one knows for certain why
> some children turn out well and others
> seem to lose their way. You did your
> best under difficult circumstances. Now
> stop punishing yourself. Good luck to
> you, dear.

In her fascinating book *The Ann Landers
Encyclopedia A to Z*, Ann mentions that "no one
knows why life must be so punishing to some of
God's finest creatures."

One of the national best-seller books today
has been *When Bad Things Happen to Good
People*, by Rabbi Harold Kushner. The book had
its beginning in 1966 when Rabbi Kushner's son
Aaron was found to have progeria, a rare
disease that drastically accelerates the aging
process. Aaron died in 1977 at the age of
fourteen. His little body was that of a small old
man.

The sickness suffered by his son threw
Rabbi Kushner into a state of shock and doubt.
How could a good God allow such horror to come
to a family that tried to walk close by his side?

For a year Rabbi Kushner wrestled with
the question in writing. The result was his book
that has proved so popular with people who have
suffered some personal tragedy and found
themselves questioning basic, long-held beliefs

---

about the goodness or even the existence of God. With utter honesty Rabbi Kushner admits that the ultimate explanation of suffering is a mystery.

In a recent edition of the *Christopher News Notes*, we are reminded that "human beings have always sought an answer to the mystery of pain. Ultimately, there are no satisfactory answers to the question of pain and suffering."

CHAPTER TWO

A Nobel Prize Winner to the Rescue

Dr. Charles H. Townes, a Nobel Prize winner in physics, gave me a new outlook on the mystery of suffering. Dr. Townes is an active church member. Besides being provost and professor of physics at the Massachusetts Institute of Technology, he finds time to instruct young people in religion.

One Sunday morning in 1964, Dr. Townes was talking with a Bible class on radio. The subject was the relationship of science and religion. Dr. Townes was urging that scientific and religious thought, far from conflicting, are today finding more and more in common, and are destined ultimately to merge.

The editors of *Think* magazine, published by IBM, were so intrigued by Dr. Townes's ideas that they asked him to develop his thoughts into an article. Dr. Townes was working on his article when word came from Stockholm that he had been awarded a Nobel Prize for his work in

---

developing the maser, which eventually led to the laser.

Dr. Townes's article, "The Convergence of Science and Religion," appeared in the March-April 1966 issue of *Think*. The article is so important, so powerful, so timely, that I wrote for permission to quote from this superb presentation.

"To me," says Dr. Townes, "science and religion are both universal, and basically very similar. In fact, to make the argument clear, I should like to adopt the rather extreme point of view that their differences are largely superficial, and that the two become almost indistinguishable if we look at the real nature of each."

Dr. Townes then goes on to show how the attitude of science has changed from nineteenth-century materialism to today when "faith is necessary to men of both science and religion."

The following is a most interesting observation by Dr. Townes: "If we compare how great scientific ideas arrive, they look remarkably like religious revelation viewed in a nonmystical way.

"Scientific knowledge, in the popular mind, comes by logical deductions or by the accumulation of data which is analyzed by established methods in order to draw generalizations called laws.

"But such a description of scientific discovery is a travesty on the real thing. Most of the important discoveries come about very differently, and are much more closely akin to revelation.

"The great scientific discoveries, the real leaps, do not usually come from the so-called 'scientific method' but by revelations which are just as real."

Dr. Townes knows whereof he speaks. The idea that led eventually to the laser came to the physicist while he was sitting on a park bench admiring some azaleas in Washington, D.C. Here, now, are golden words from Dr. Townes.

He tells us that in both religion and science "we must expect paradoxes, and not be surprised or unduly troubled by them. We know of paradoxes in physics, such as those concerning the nature of light.

"In the realm of religion, we are troubled by the suffering around us and its apparent inconsistency with a God of love. Such paradoxes do not destroy our faith. They simply remind us of a limited understanding."

Some people act as though the mystery of suffering is the only unknown in our lives. The solemn truth is that we are completely surrounded by mysteries on all sides. If only we become aware of this fact then the mystery of suffering will take its rightful place, as a part of the mysterious universe, which we do not understand.

The late Dr. Wernher von Braun was known as "The Father of the *Saturn V* Rocket" that took our astronauts to the moon. Von Braun was considered to be the greatest rocket expert of our space age. In a commencement address, which he gave at St. Louis University in St. Louis, Missouri, Von Braun emphasized the fact that nature around us harbors thousands of more mysteries than it does answers.

You may have heard people say that they have trouble with their faith because they cannot visualize God. The answer Von Braun gives to this objection is superb:

"Can a physicist visualize an electron? The electron is materially inconceivable, and yet it is so perfectly known through its effects that we use it to illuminate our cities, guide our airliners through the night skies, and take the most accurate measurements.

"What strange rationale makes some physicists accept the inconceivable electron as real while refusing to accept the reality of God on the ground that they cannot conceive him?"

How strange to realize that the electron has never been seen by man. We believe in it for the same reason we should believe in God — because of the effects we notice in the universe around us.

Perhaps you say that when you turn on your electric light you "see electricity." The truth is that we never see the electrons forcing their way through the tungsten wire that makes up the filament of the lamp.

Do you know why the light bulbs in your home are called incandescent lamps? The word "incandescent" means "glowing white-hot." And this is exactly what happens. The electricity going through the very thin wires, or filaments, in the lamps makes them glow white-hot, so they give off light as well as heat.

"But," you may object, "I most certainly see electrons in motion when I see a flash of lightning."

When you look at a lightning flash, you do not see electricity itself. All you see is a burning spark channel or burning column of air that may be about an inch in diameter, or even as thin as a hair on your head. The path of this burning air column may be as long as ten miles. The searing, three-thousand-degree heat of the flash causes the channel of air to expand or explode with tremendous force. The airwave thus produced beats against your eardrum to cause the sensation we call thunder. If the discharge is close by, the thunder comes as a sharp whiplike crack.

The comments of Von Braun on the unseen electron may be made even more vivid for you if you consider the following. Let me begin by asking: "What are you looking at right now?"

"I'm looking at print on this paper," you reply. Your answer seems clear-cut, definite, and final. The scientist, however, will inform you that your answer has not even dipped into the magic, mystery, and fascination that swirls through this page.

According to atomic theory, this print, this paper, even the tip of your ear, and indeed your whole body, are made of atoms.

Atoms — so the theory goes — are like tiny solar systems made up of protons and electrons. The protons are in the center of the atom just as our sun is in the center of our solar system. Electrons revolve around the protons just as planets revolve around our sun.

A negative charge of electricity is called an electron and is designated by a minus sign (-). A positive charge of electricity is called a proton and is designated by a plus sign (+).

What now do scientists ask you to believe? That this paper is made up of electrical charges of electricity, which we designate by plus signs and minus signs!

Yet you and I and the scientist know that *if* we could climb down into the heart of an atom, we certainly would never expect to find plus signs and minus signs running around.

Just *what* would we see? No one knows. We are lost in mystery. We are so ignorant of what an atom really is, so ignorant of what electricity is, that we have to resort to the clumsy use of a minus sign (-) to represent what we call an electron, and a plus sign (+) to represent what we call a proton. Since we don't know what an atom really is, we invent a theory, which is nothing but an educated guess.

The most popular and well-known theory of the atom today is the Bohr theory, named after the famed Niels Bohr, Nobel Prize winner. This is the theory we have considered in this chapter. Today, however, there are scientists who wish to introduce changes into Bohr's theory.

Isaac Asimov, a well-known writer on science, reminds us, "Of course, nobody can say what the inside of an atom looks like. Conditions are so different within the atom from the conditions found in the ordinary world about us that we have nothing that will serve as a true comparison."

When you look at your big toe, you see nothing that strikes you as romantic or mysterious. To the atomic scientist, however, each square centimeter of your toe or the tip of your finger is teeming with mystery. In each cell in your body is a "universe in miniature" — a fascinating world of "planet" electrons whirling around protons.

At the convocation commemorating the one hundred twenty-fifth anniversary of the founding of the University of Notre Dame, Lee

A. DuBridge reminded his distinguished audience of the limitation of human knowledge, not only in science, but in other fields as well.

DuBridge has the experience that enables him to speak with authority. He was president of the California Institute of Technology, the institution that manages the world-famous Jet Propulsion Laboratory for the National Aeronautics and Space Administration.

"I could easily spend fifty years studying about the universe," said DuBridge, "and still not know all I'd like to know. Why? For one simple reason: If I really were intent on learning all there was to know about physics, for example, or astronomy, or biology, or economics, or philosophy, I would soon come to some question for which *nobody had any answers*.

"How many elementary particles are there? Nobody knows. How does the DNA molecule govern the development of a newborn creature? No one fully knows. Why do men and nations always fight each other? *We don't know!*"

Dr. James Van Allen is the famed scientist of the University of Iowa who discovered the Van Allen radiation belts that surround the earth, and which are named in his honor.

"At the frontier of science," says Dr. Van Allen, "the effort is subjective, intuitive, controversial, sometimes courageous, often misdirected, often inconclusive, often plain wrong."

He continues: "It is anything but exact. There are no authoritative proclamations in science. The terms conjecture, assumption, and presumption are common ones."

According to Ray Bradbury, "Science is no more than an investigation of a miracle we can never explain, and art is an interpretation of that miracle."

Dr. Ira M. Freeman is a distinguished professor of physics at Rutgers University, New Brunswick, New Jersey. With utmost honesty he admits that "physics is a purely experiential science and if it is asked *why* something is true, it can only answer that this is required by natural law. The falling of a stone can be attributed to gravitation, but it makes no sense to ask further how this force of attraction comes about, because the laws of nature themselves cannot be explained."

As it has already been pointed out, your body is a bundle of negative charges and positive charges. *How* do these electrons and protons come together to make *you*?

Your body is made up of elements that are quite lifeless in themselves — iron, nitrogen, phosphorus, calcium, etc. Yet — behold the miracle! — each simple element is linked to another until the final organization can think, work, talk, and read this print. Who can explain it? Who can tell you why?

The mystery of life lies in the way a few kinds of atoms combine into thousands of different molecules, and in the way these molecules organize to make a living cell — and a living person.

All living things are made of protoplasm. But just *what* is protoplasm? Scientists have identified the ingredients of protoplasm. It consists of 62 percent oxygen, 20 percent carbon, 10 percent hydrogen, 3 percent nitrogen, 2.5 percent calcium, 1.14 percent phosphorus, plus a small amount of additional elements.

But here is the baffling thing: Even though a scientist goes to his lab and measures out the exact percentages of each element, and mixes thoroughly, he has *not* been able, so far, to get protoplasm. He has *not* been able to get living matter. Why not?

There is something *more* to life than matter. But what? How is it possible that the same atoms you find in rocks and air are arranged in such a way in us so that we live and breathe?

In their beautiful textbook on biology entitled *Life and the Molecule*, the authors Navarra, Zafforoni, and Garone ask, "What is life?" To which they reply, "There is no easy answer to this question. Life and what it is, is one of the most puzzling mysteries of science."

Some scientists inform us that the dimensions of human knowledge are dwarfed by the dimensions of human ignorance. Among these scientists is Dr. Leonard Jefferson, a member of the Holy Spirit Parish in Palmyra, Pennsylvania. He is a recipient of the Lilly Award for outstanding and original diabetes research. According to Dr. Jefferson, "The more you learn about the human body and how it functions, the more in awe you are of the complexity that is beyond the comprehension of the human mind."

Dr. Robert J. White is one of the world's experts on the human brain and nervous system. He is a lifelong Catholic who is sensitive to the relationship between science and religion. He is a professor at the Case-Western Reserve University medical school and director of neurological surgery at Cleveland Metropolitan General Hospital.

"Trying to unravel the mysteries of the brain," says Dr. White, "has put me more than ever in awe of the brain. No matter how much we learn about the brain, we can never expect to explain the mind completely.

"What," asks Professor White, "is intelligence? We are light years away from knowing what intelligence is. We can try to define it with comparisons; we cannot say what it consists of. You study the brain of a genius, and it doesn't show anything different from the brain of an idiot. Their tissue is the same, their brain waves travel in the same way.

"No chemical analysis, no electrical presence separates those two individuals. In a scientific laboratory, you'll never discover why one person can write so well or paint so well or do mathematics so well, and another cannot."

Sir Isaac Newton is thought of as one of the greatest scientists of all times. The world paid him honor for all he did to bring to light new ideas, and to thank him for his work in advancing science. Yet, in spite of his great knowledge, here is what Newton said of himself: "I do not know what I may appear to the world, but to myself I seem to have been like a boy playing on the seashore . . . now and then finding a smoother pebble or a prettier shell than ordinary, while the great ocean of truth lay all undiscovered before me."

At a science symposium held at the University of Wisconsin, Dr. Milton O. Pella, professor of science education at the university, pointed out again and again, "There is now more unknown than known."

In recent years Jacques Piccard made a voyage for one month in the experimental submarine *Ben Franklin* in the Gulf Stream, that great "river in the Atlantic Ocean" which flows north from the Gulf of Mexico. Hundreds of feet below the surface of the Atlantic Ocean the *Ben Franklin*, with six men aboard, drifted silently northward with the flow of the Gulf Stream, from Florida to Massachusetts. With its engines cut off, the submarine moved with the current without rising to the surface. From viewing windows man got a new look at the mysterious ocean.

After the voyage, Jacques Piccard said, "The Gulf Stream has been deeply studied and a few secrets have been uncovered. But it will probably always shield the majority of its mysteries from man.

"This is the law of universal science," continued Piccard. "The deeper you delve into it, the more you realize that it is endless, limitless, infinite."

By reputation and accomplishment, Dr. Lewis Thomas is a leader in the field of medical practice and research. He is the author of an acclaimed series of essays on man and nature, life and death, sickness and health. His book *The Lives of a Cell: Notes of a Biology Watcher* won the 1975 National Book Award in arts and letters.

Currently president of the Memorial Sloan-Kettering Cancer Center, Dr. Thomas was formerly dean of the Yale Medical School, and before that chairman of the departments of pathology and medicine and dean at the New York University Bellevue Medical Center.

Here, now, are the words of a man who is researching as well as administering one of the country's prestigious medical centers: "I am a mystified man. I don't really understand very much. I can't imagine any terminal point where everyone will breathe a sigh and will say, 'Now we understand the whole thing.' It's going to remain beyond us."

One of the mysteries that overwhelms Dr. Thomas is how the human brain comes into existence from what was at one point a single embryonic cell. "People," he says, "ought to be walking around all day, all through their waking hours, calling to each other in endless wonderment, talking of nothing except that cell."

Many years ago, on a beautiful day in June, I began to paint a white picket fence that ran along the east side of my dad's backyard. Alas, a portion of the fence was covered with morning-glory vines. As I pulled the vines loose, I noticed that each vine twisted itself around its support in a counterclockwise direction.

This is the same direction that water whirlpools down the drain in a kitchen sink. And, on a calm day, smoke spirals or twists upward from a chimney in the same counterclockwise fashion. To my amazement, when I was in Australia, I found that the twist was in the opposite direction. Upon my arrival in Sydney on Saturday, July 25, 1970, I stood by the sink in my hotel room and watched in wonder as the water swirled down the drain in a clockwise motion.

But *why* does this happen? In his fascinating book *This Hill, This Valley* Hal Borland reminds us that there are laws of nature we most likely will never understand.

It is all very well to say that the twisting of vines and the whirling of water are the result of the turning of the earth. These, however, are facts, not ultimate answers. That is the *way* things happen, not *why* they happen.

Is a wild morning glory aware of the turning of the earth? Is a pole bean so endowed with this knowledge that I cannot force it to twist the other way?

"There is," says Hal Borland, "some law beyond, some way of life, some necessity in nature that I can recognize but not wholly understand."

We and Rip Van Winkle have a lot in common. Both we and Rip share a common achievement — we have slept or will have slept one-third of our lives away. Unlikely as it sounds, by the time we are sixty, we will have slept more than twenty years. The time is spread out, of course, to an average of eight hours a day, seven days a week.

The old saying "sleep tight" is bad advice. If we followed it we would wake up as stiff as a board. During an average night's sleep, we jerk, turn over, twitch, kick, make faces, and mumble once every ten minutes or thereabouts.

The deepest sleep occurs in the first ninety minutes. After this period, it tapers off into "dream sleep." Contrary to popular belief, almost everyone dreams two or three hours each night. Shorter dreams last about ten minutes. Toward morning these dreams become longer.

Why do we sleep? Though sleep is one of man's most familiar experiences, it is one of his deeper mysteries. Scientists so far have been unable to find the answer to this basic question.

Recent research projects have put to rest many long established "facts" — actually myths — about sleep. But still there is little that modern sleep experts agree on.

If we followed the popular medical advice of the Middle Ages about how to sleep better, we would have our heads shaved, be bled to an anemic white, then gorge ourselves with a mixture of wild carrot, parsley, and peony seeds.

Only one thing is certain, and it can be summed up neatly and almost absurdly: Human beings sleep better when they lie down.

The more we study, the more we find that reality is much more complex and more puzzling than we ever imagined. Each new question that is answered opens up a whole universe of new questions. It is like opening a door, only to find ourselves looking down a long corridor with many doors on both sides waiting to be opened, and these doors, in turn, lead to more corridors, and more doors.

The rocks brought back from the moon, for example, reveal that none of the theories developed to explain the moon are adequate, and the moon itself, shining up there in the night sky is, if anything, a greater mystery than it ever was before, now that we have captured a few pounds of its substance.

On Sunday evening, August 26, 1979, Senator William Proxmire spoke at Creighton University. He informed his audience that he had given his Golden Fleece Award recently to show his objection to a National Science Foundation grant of $84,000 to psychologists who were trying to find out why we fall in love. Senator Proxmire said that he objected to this waste of the taxpayer's money "because no one — not even the National Science Foundation — can argue that falling in love is a science. Why a man falls in love with a woman, and vice versa, is a mystery."

A very delightful mystery, I might add. So much so, in fact, that the British novelist and playwright Charles Morgan said, "There is no surprise more magical than the surprise of being loved. It is the finger of God on a man's shoulder."

What scientists don't know about some basic matters would fill an encyclopedia. That's what two Britons, Ronald Duncan and Miranda Weston-Smith, learned when they teamed up to edit a most unusual book called *Encyclopaedia of Ignorance.*

For some twenty centuries, encyclopedists from Pliny to the editors of *Encyclopaedia Britannica* have collected and recorded all that was known. But "compared to the pond of knowledge," say the British editors, "our ignorance remains atlantic."

Over half a hundred distinguished scientists were delighted to take part. They responded eagerly with essays that sum up what is known — and unknown — in their fields. The interesting thing was that the more eminent the scientists were, the more ready they were to run to the editors with their ignorance.

Despite our continual rise from the depths of ignorance, we realize more and more how much is still a mystery to us. Some of the most tantalizing mysteries are those found in our own bodies. What, for example, causes a person to age? Because scientists don't know what causes cells to break down with age, they can't say that anything causes longevity.

Science can often catalog events it cannot explain. When a man is thirty, for example, his body has just passed its peak. It has started dying a little every day, losing about one percent of its functional capacity every year.

Cells are disappearing, tissues are stiffening, chemical reactions are slowing down. By 70 his body temperature will be two degrees lower. He will stand an inch or so shorter, and have longer ears. His nose will grow half an inch wider, and another half an inch longer. The hair on a man's head is thickest at about 20; after that each hair shrinks, and by 70 his hairs are as fine as they were when he was a baby.

At the age of 30 about 70 pounds of a 175-pound man are muscle. Over the next 40 years he loses 10 pounds of that muscle as cells stop reproducing and die. His shoulders narrow an inch. The remaining muscles grow weaker as the fibers become frayed, jumbled, and riddled with deposits of waste material. His strength peaks at about 30 and then steadily diminishes.

One of the most startling facts is that for every 100 American men age 65 and over today, there are 146 women of the same age. Back in the 1930s men and women lived to be about the same age. For reasons yet unclear, the life expectancy of women made a spectacular jump over that of men. By 1978, women could expect to live 77.2 years, men 69.5 years. From 1960 to 1970 the number of women 65 and over rose at twice the rate of men of the same age.

Many doctors wish that their patients realized that mysteries are found even in medicine itself. Because people fail to recognize that medicine is not an exact science, frustration, disappointment, and lawsuits result when there is a failure.

Dr. Harold Bursztajn, in cooperation with others from the Harvard University medical establishment, has recently published a book called *Medical Choices, Medical Chances*. The authors of this book claim that patients and doctors should level together about every medical decision. They emphasize that "there are no absolute guarantees for cure or comfort. Every medical decision is a gamble and the stakes are high. To work together effectively, both doctor and patient must acknowledge that they are gambling and not perpetuate the illusion of total certainty. Contemporary scientific thought encourages the mutual acknowledgment of uncertainty and opens the door to honest medical care."

By now, no doubt, you will agree that it will be easier to accept the mystery of suffering if we stop to realize that in our everyday world untold mysteries swirl around us on all sides.

When I think of some of the many mysteries that surround us, I'm reminded of the comments of an astronomy professor from Florida. When asked what he thought heaven would be like, he replied, "After spending my life pondering the mysteries of existence and the universe, I expect heaven will be a place where I can say, 'Okay, I give up. What *was* the answer?' "

CHAPTER THREE

Why Job Stopped Screaming

If you read the book of Job you will
find that in the first part of the book,
Job screams out to God in anger. By
the end of the book, Job has become a patient
man.

What made the change? Job received a
much needed education. He was led to see that
suffering is but one of the many, many
mysteries that surround us on every side. If we
can't solve the mysteries behind events in our
physical world, how can we ever hope to find an
answer to the more complicated mystery in our
spiritual world?

Since Job did not have a Dr. Charles H.
Townes or a Dr. Wernher von Braun to give him
a needed education in the facts of life, God
himself took up this task of educating Job.

It is interesting to note how God set about
this undertaking. God did not begin by blasting
Job for his outburst of anger. God does not hurl
insults at Job and claim that Job's ignorance is

equaled only by his arrogance. God did not call Job a balsa-brained parallelepiped or a cabbagehead. Instead, God begins his instruction in low gear. He asks Job a series of seemingly innocent, simple questions. Put into a modern scenario, the script might read something like this:

GOD: "What keeps the earth moving in its path in the heavens?"

JOB: "I don't know, Lord. It is a mystery to me!"

GOD: "What causes the sun to give forth light?"

JOB: "I don't know, Lord. It is a mystery to me!"

GOD: "How do the birds of the air know how to navigate across vast distances?"

JOB: "I don't know, Lord. It is a mystery to me!"

GOD: "Since you don't understand the mysteries behind simple physical events that surround you on all sides, how do you expect to understand the far greater mystery behind the problem of suffering?"

By now, Job caught the idea that was summed up by Dr. Charles H. Townes many centuries later, and that is: We live in a universe of mystery and paradoxes, the greatest of which is suffering. "Such paradoxes do not destroy our faith. They simply remind us of a limited understanding."

Today we know no more than Job did concerning the mystery of suffering. The one thing we do know, however, is the truth uttered by the lips of St. Paul, ". . . the sufferings of this present time are not worth comparing with the glory that is to be revealed to us" (Romans 8:18).

"The genuine Christian," declared the late Cardinal Albert G. Meyer of Chicago, "cannot be a pessimist. His must always be the idealism which enables him to believe, to hope, to know that no matter how wicked the world may be, no matter how hopeless it may all seem, he always possesses the secret of true happiness here as well as hereafter: Jesus Christ, Son of God made man. The spiritual joy of the Christian is found in God. 'I go to prepare a place for you that where I am, you also may be.' (John 14:3) This is the promise of Christ."

In his beautiful Easter sermon, Father Walter J. Burghardt, S.J., professor of theology, Woodstock College, said, "The Christian is as much alive to pain and suffering as anyone else, but he realizes the glorious truth — the Resurrection means that one day we will live with Christ in happiness."

Michael Kent captures this truly beautiful Christian spirit in his inspiring book, *The Mass of Brother Michel.* On the eve of their execution, Michel says to Louise, "Tomorrow we lay aside these garments we have worn on earth, and in their place what glory we receive! Tomorrow heaven is ours, and beauty, and end of pain, forever. I cannot think what it will be like to live without pain, but tomorrow it will be as if it had never been. And in proportion as we have suffered on earth for love, so much greater will our joy be in heaven."

On one happy day in the future we will enter into the joy of our heavenly home. On that day all the clocks and calendars will have finished their counting. Together with our loved ones, we will rejoice for always. No wonder the poet Phoebe Cary said:

> One sweetly solemn thought
>   Comes to me o'er and o'er;
> I am nearer home today
>   Than I ever have been before;
> Nearer my Father's house,
>   Where the many mansions be;
> Nearer the great white throne,
>   Nearer the crystal sea;
> Nearer the bound of life,
>   Where we lay our burdens down;
> Nearer leaving the cross,
>   Nearer gaining the crown!

On August 15, 1982, my friend Father Ed Farren celebrated his fiftieth year as a Jesuit. His views are expressed in the following letter:

> Grow old along with me!
> The best is yet to be,

> The last of life, for which the
> first was made.

> These are the opening words of
> Robert Browning's poem "Rabbi Ben
> Ezra." I learned them when I was a
> young college student, and although
> they impressed me even then, now that
> I am getting old they impress me even
> more.

> For a Christian, death is not
> something terrible, but in the words of
> the Mass for the dead, death means:
> "life is changed, and not taken away."
> This life is but a preparation for a
> better life. In the life that I look
> forward to, "The best is yet to be, the
> last of life, for which the first was
> made."

A nineteen-year-old Polish boy was stricken with a fatal sickness. When informed that he would not recover and that death was fast approaching, the boy was not in the least saddened. Rather, his face glowed with calmness and happiness. Echoing the words of the psalmist, he exclaimed: "I rejoice at the things that are told unto me. We shall go into the house of the Lord."

Like this young man, St. Stanislaus, we too should rejoice at the things that are told us. For we also are to enter into the house of the Lord.

Each day sees us nearer this heavenly home.

A few winters ago the newspapers carried the account of Donald Redfearn, an attractive little blond boy, dying from bone cancer in East St. Louis. When visitors came to the Illinois hospital to see him, one of them asked whether he was saddened by the thought of death. Looking up from his hospital bed, Donald replied, "When I think of dying and going to heaven to see God, I can hardly wait."

Perhaps you agree that we are "Easter people," and a vision of heaven is ours; but in the barbed-wire world of sharp reality, when the sledgehammer blows of suffering and disaster hit us and our loved ones, they pound us into the dust.

The agony of watching a loved one suffer is so devastating, we would rather suffer the pain ourselves, if only our loved ones could go free.

When I was a young boy in the Immaculate Conception grade school in Butte, Montana, I used to wonder why our Blessed Mother was spoken of as the Mother of Sorrows. After all, it was Christ who was nailed to the cross, not Mary. Alas, with the passing years, I found that being forced to simply "stand by" and watch a loved one suffer is the most excruciating pain of all.

Now and then you read in the newspapers that torrents of rain crash pell-mell on California hillsides. The result — gravity pulls down and creates an overwhelming mud slide. When the many afflictions of life beat down upon our loved ones, the result may be that the suffering pulls us down into a mud slide of despair and depression.

At such times, according to Dr. James C. Dobson, "Nothing could be more dangerous than to permit our emotions to rule our destinies. To do so is to be cast adrift in the path of life's storms."

Dr. Dobson is an educator and an expert in the field of human relations and child development. He is also a widely respected authority on marriage and family life as well as a committed Christian husband and father. He is host of the nationally syndicated television and radio show *Focus on the Family*.

Dr. Dobson warns us that if we permit our emotions to rule us, we have become mere slaves to our feelings.

The first principle of mental health is to accept that which cannot be changed. We can easily go to pieces over the adverse circumstances beyond our control. We can also resolve to withstand them. We can will to hang tough, or we can yield to cowardice. Depression is often evidence of emotional surrender.

Since we are human beings we are limited in energy and ability. If we allow ourselves to run down, we can be of no use to those we love, and so, the necessity of taking everything with the least commotion possible.

We owe it both to our loved ones — and ourselves — not to become quagmired in a swamp of black thoughts. It requires a determined act of our will and an act of faith in God's wisdom to leap up from the dismal swamp and soar on the wings of hope and trust into the blue sky.

As children of God we have the confidence that all things that God allows will somehow work together for good. That good is often hidden from our eyes at present, but in the light of heaven above, we shall know the truth.

It is interesting to note that Mary is called the Mother of Sorrows, but not the Mother of Sadness. Rather she has been called, "The Lady with the smiling eyes and the singing heart." The melody of the Magnificat wove itself through the framework of her life like a morning glory entwining a trellis. Despite the sword of sorrow that pierced Mary's heart, the song continued, ". . . my spirit rejoices in God my Savior, . . . for he who is mighty has done great things for me" (Luke 1:47, 49).

The joy of spirit that should be ours will not cause us to burst geyserlike into song, turn cartwheels, or even smile like the Mona Lisa. Our hearts may be as heavy as stone and as dark as evening shadows.

True Christians are those who learn the

lesson of joy in sorrow; even though sorrow may be squeezing our hearts in a steel-jawed vise of pain, our joy is strictly an intellectual conviction that God must have some reason for allowing such dreadful suffering — a reason hidden deep from us, and one we will understand only in the light of the great white throne of God.

Many years ago, in one of his retreats, Father Vincent McCorry mentioned that there are peaks of satisfaction in every human life, and it is usually in connection with these high moments of existence that we use the strong word "happiness." We speak of the happiness of a bride, or of a proud mother, or the winner of a scholarship. But these strong joys are likewise rare joys. It is not really pertinent to ask an ordinary man on an ordinary day whether or not he is happy. Yet on an ordinary day an ordinary man ought to be ordinarily content. People need not regularly shout for joy or habitually throw their hats in the air, but they should be at least normally contented. A person should be "happy in his vocation," not enthusiastic perhaps, but fundamentally satisfied. Obviously, fundamental satisfaction may coexist with accidental dissatisfaction.

If we are like most people, we most likely complain that the "great moments" of life are all too few, and they are separated by long, flat, dusty deserts of monotony.

One young man felt so helpless and

overwhelmed by the disasters that blew in upon him, he spent his last paycheck to make a trip home to visit his dad.

On the final evening of their visit, the two men were standing on the west Florida shore, watching the sun sink into the Gulf of Mexico. The young man, unable to contain his bitterness any longer, said, "You know, Dad, if we could take all the great moments we experience in our lifetimes and put them back to back, they wouldn't last twenty minutes."

The father's simple reply was, "Yup." The young man turned to his dad, stunned. His dad was still rapt in attention, studying the sun that was perched on the horizon. Then, looking evenly into his son's eyes, the father added quietly, "Precious, aren't they?"

No wonder the poet Sara Teasdale tells us:

> Spend all you have for loveliness,
>   Buy it, and never count the cost;
> For one white singing hour of peace
>   Count many a year of strife well lost,
> And for a breath of ecstasy
>   Give all you have been, or could be.

The saints knew how to take the bitter with the sweet. They praised God for the joys when he chose to send them, and these temporal consolations made them realize more keenly the joys of heaven. They looked forever at the bright side because this is God's side, and they wished to see all things with the eyes of God.

"Thee, God, I come from. To thee go." This is the Christian philosophy of life. With this philosophy you can take. . .

> The heartache, and the thousand natural shocks
> That flesh is heir to . . . the whips and scorns of time,
> The oppressor's wrong, the proud man's contumely,
> The pangs of despised love, and law's delay,
> The insolence of office, and the spurns
> That patient merit of the unworthy takes.
>
> > Shakespeare —
> > *Hamlet*, III, i (62-74)

Without this philosophy, you will complain with Maurice Maeterlinck, "The ant is far less unhappy than the very happiest of men." "All seek happiness and receive only death."

If you wish to capture the bluebird of happiness that eluded Maurice Maeterlinck, you will have to learn the truth Ann Blyth received from her mother: "She taught me that faith was the only sound foundation for lasting joy."

In his inspiring book *Achieving Peace of Heart*, Father Narciso Irala, S.J., reminds us, "God wants us to be happy. He repeats it a thousand times in Scripture and Liturgy. Joy is possible. How? By shifting your gaze from the unpleasant aspect, from the ugly face of suffering, and concentrating on the bright side."

Rather than waste our time bemoaning the disappointments and sufferings that come into our lives, we should focus our attention on the many good things God gives us. To put it in a more poetic way, we can either complain because rosebushes have thorns, or rejoice because they have such beautiful flowers.

The fact that we are "Easter people" does not take away the pain, nor does it banish the cross. It does give us a reason to accept suffering in a spirit of patience and with the blessed hope of happy days to come. It is up to us, however, to focus on the roses, not on the thorns.

Reinhold Niebuhr has given us these golden words: "God, grant me the serenity to accept the things I cannot change, courage to change the things I can, and wisdom to know the difference." No wonder they are such a source of comfort to those in Alcoholics Anonymous.

"Though friendship and peace with God is the foundation of true happiness," remarked Father Edward Garesché, "yet something more is required, as is quite plain from the fact that many good, pious people seem scarcely to have acquired the art of being happy.

"What is this further accomplishment? Is it

not to be found in the practice of looking on the bright side of things?

"The dark side is unhappily often but too obtrusive, while the brighter side requires looking for and needs some effort to discover. One must acquire the unvarying habit of looking always for the bright side of everything, if one would learn and practice thoroughly the art of being happy.

"See in each individual occurrence as much as you can that which is cheerful, encouraging, and good. Turn back, as far as possible, on the gloomy and discouraging aspects of things."

It is said that the best remedy for discontent is to count your blessings.

G.K. Chesterton, when he wrote his autobiography near the end of a long and useful life, set himself the task of defining in a single sentence the most important lesson he had learned. He concluded that the critical thing was whether one took things for granted or took them with gratitude.

According to Father John Powell, our vision — that is, the way we interpret and evaluate reality — is the key to our emotional and mental health. The theory is that our perceptions cause our emotions and affect our behavior. Consequently, we must begin with our thinking, with the way we are seeing things, with our vision. We must keep in mind that our ideas and attitudes generate our emotional response.

In his timely and inspirational book *Fully Human, Fully Alive*, Father John Powell informs us, "Fully alive people find enjoyment in what others regard as drudgery or duty. They are aware of the thorns, but concentrate on the roses."

It is incredible how a point of view and mind-set determine what one sees on one's horizon. For example, three people look at the same sunset; but because of their different points of view, their thoughts scamper in three different directions.

- The artist feels the beauty of nature exploding in a million colors. He can almost hear the colors clashing, diminishing, and finally dying.
- The bus driver flicks on his headlights. He knows the driving will be rougher and he'll have to be more attentive.
- The owner of a discotheque sees business pulling in. He's thinking in terms of dollars and decimal points, investment and profit, dancing and drinks.

The mind definitely influences our lives in a lot more ways than we realize — right down to whether we choose to complain to God because of the little crosses we must bear, or to rejoice because God has allowed those crosses in our lives so that we can help those who are burdened with heavier ones.

CHAPTER FOUR

From Blind Milton to the Jungle Doctor

When astronaut William Anders orbited the moon on Christmas Eve of 1968, he looked back two hundred forty thousand miles away and saw planet earth floating like a delicate Christmas tree ornament in the vast ocean of space.

"It was," said the astronaut, "small, finite, and limited; actually, rather puny when compared to the vast blackness through which it drifted." This experience reminded Anders "that we are all brothers — riders together on a small planet."

It will help us on our journey through time and space if we stop to consider how some of our fellow passengers have met the problem of pain and suffering.

The poet John Milton lost his sight when he was about fifty. He became impatient with himself, and wondered whether God would not also lose patience with him, since his service to God was now necessarily limited. As Jacob

---

wrestled with the angel, Milton's struggle likewise ended in a blessing, which is expressed in the last line of his poem:

> When I consider how my light is spent,
> Ere half my days, in this dark world and
> wide,
> And that one talent which is death to hide
> Lodged with me useless, though my soul
> more bent
> To serve therewith my Maker, and
> present
> My true account, lest he returning chide,
> "Doth God exact day-labor, light denied?"
>
> That murmur, soon replies, "God doth
> not need
> Either man's work or his own gifts. Who
> best
> Bear his mild yoke, they serve him best.
> His state
> Is kingly: thousands at his bidding speed,
> And post o'er land and ocean without
> rest;
> They also serve who only stand and
> wait."

Baseball fans may recall the name Roy Campanella. He was the former star catcher of the old Brooklyn Dodgers. Three times he was chosen as the National League's most valuable player. He assisted the team in five World

Series games. He was elected into the Baseball Hall of Fame in 1969.

Roy recalls that terrible night of January 27, 1958, when the car he was driving skidded on ice and crashed into a telephone pole. The impact threw him under the dashboard, breaking his neck. Emergency surgery saved his life, but his spinal cord had been severed; he was paralyzed from the shoulders down. His life changed quickly from athlete to paralytic.

"If there was a time to quit, it was then . . . but I didn't," Roy said, referring to the accident. "I accepted the wheelchair." He described desire, dedication, hard work, and determination as better than medication in his struggle to lead an active life.

Twenty-two years after the accident, "Campy," as he's affectionately known to baseball fans, was nominated for the Tau Award from the Sacred Heart Rehabilitation Hospital in Milwaukee, Wisconsin. The award was presented to Campy at a dinner at the Hyatt-Regency Hotel.

Campy beamed as he was praised for his services and commitment to the disabled. "It means so much to me after being a quadraplegic for twenty-two years to realize that I have been of help to others." Campy's advice to handicapped people is simple: "Follow the good voice from within and 'think right.' "

One of the most inspiring gospel singers of

our times is Merrill Womach. On Thanksgiving Day, 1961, he was flying alone, piloting a two-engine propeller plane. Ice choked off the engines. The plane crashed in the woods just fifty yards from the Beaver Marsh, Oregon, airfield.

Immediately after the crash, more than one hundred gallons of fuel the plane was carrying exploded, engulfing Womach in flames as he stumbled toward a road. His face was burned beyond recognition.

More than fifty operations later and with the help of what he calls "a simple, childlike faith in a great God," Womach was almost back to normal in appearance and all the way back in business. An important part of Womach's message is that "Christians aren't exempt from or removed from problems."

The gospel singer said his long-standing faith never wavered because of his accident. Nor did he question why God would allow such suffering or such a condition that will require regular skin grafts for the rest of his life. "I've never questioned why God let it happen," Womach said. "I just know there's a purpose and a plan."

The examples afforded us by Roy Campanella and Merrill Womach give proof to the words of St. Peter, ". . . You may for a time have to suffer the distress of many trials: but this is so that your faith, which is more precious than the passing splendor of fire-tried gold, may by its genuineness lead to praise, glory, and honor when Jesus Christ appears" (1 Peter 1:6-7).

Because of Christ's resurrection, says St. Peter, we have been given a new birth, a birth unto hope, a birth to an imperishable inheritance that is kept in heaven for us. "There is cause for rejoicing here" (1 Peter 1:6).

There is no way to avoid suffering. It is up to us to give it eternal value by accepting it with equanimity of soul for the love of God. We can learn to accept life for what it is — a mixed bag, so to speak — and take each day as it comes.

A young assistant pastor went to visit a woman whose five-year-old daughter was dying of cancer. As he looked down on the dying child, the young priest felt utterly inept and helpless. All the words he had planned to say went in a swallow down his throat.

When the young priest returned to the rectory, he told the pastor his embarrassing experience. "What should I have said," he asked the older priest, "to give some meaning to this suffering?"

"You did the right thing by not saying anything," counseled the older man, "since none of us understands suffering any better than she does. Just being with her, and in your loving care for her, you shared something of her suffering. If there is any meaning to be found in suffering, it will be found in that."

Pope Paul VI, nearing the end of his life and quite aware that death was fast approaching, gave us his views on life. "Everything has been a gift. Despite its pains, its obscure mysteries, its sufferings, its inevitable decay, this mortal life is something very beautiful, a prodigy always original and moving, an event which deserves to be chanted in joy. Behind life, behind nature, behind the universe, there is intelligence, and there is Love."

Father Mike Hughes is a victim of cystic fibrosis. He has also developed diabetes, for which he takes insulin. A bout of mononucleosis incapacitated him for three months a couple of years ago. On bad days he is plagued by a persistent cough, stomach upset, troubled breathing, and diarrhea.

"Faith doesn't explain suffering," he says, "but gives a reason for it in the sense that we have somewhere better to go. We have a reason for living, but a reason for dying too. This is one of the greatest gifts of faith."

An interesting anecdote on how to face suffering is given to us by Billie Wilcox. While she and her husband, Frank, were living in Pakistan many years ago, their six-month-old baby died. An old Punjabi who heard of their grief came to comfort them.

"A tragedy like this is similar to being

plunged into boiling water," he explained. "If you are an egg, your affliction will make you hard-boiled and unresponsive. If you are a potato, you will emerge soft and pliable, resilient and adaptable."

"It may sound funny to God," said Billie Wilcox, "but there have been many times when I have prayed, 'O Lord, let me be a potato.'"

Did you ever reflect on the fact that it is only because the oyster has overcome an irritating problem that we have the pearl? When an irritant, such as a grain of sand, gets inside an oyster, and the oyster can't get rid of it, the smart oyster does the next best thing: He surrounds the irritant with a material that becomes a pearl!

If some irritant enters into our lives, we can imitate the example of the oyster. Make a pearl of it. It may have to be a pearl of patience, but, anyhow, make it a pearl. It takes faith and love to do this.

It is interesting to see how some of the outstanding saints faced the problems that came into their lives. St. Jane Frances de Chantal is honored by the Church for being a wife, mother, widow, and foundress of a religious community for women.

This extraordinary woman experienced family problems both great and small. Her first three babies died soon after birth. She then bore four healthy children: a son and three daughters. Shortly after the last birth, however, her husband was shot in the thigh in a hunting accident. Botched surgery resulted in his death a few days later.

The young widow fell into a deep depression, neglecting her children and refusing to forgive the man who was responsible for the accident. Finally a letter from her father helped Jane overcome her grief. Her father reminded Jane of her responsibilities to her children and her Christian duty to forgive. Gradually recovering from her depression, Jane went on to become one of the most remarkable saints the Church has ever seen.

Dr. Tom Dooley is known as the jungle doctor who brought medical care to thousands in Indochina during the 1950s. Following his graduation from St. Louis University Medical School in 1953, Dooley began his medical work as a U.S. Navy doctor in Vietnam. He co-founded Medical International Cooperation, a nonprofit, nonsectarian organization for gathering money, equipment, and personnel for seven hospitals in Asia, Africa, and South America.

Dooley brought medical care to backward areas where often there was not even one doctor per two hundred thousand people. His Asian patients, much to his dismay, literally worshiped him. Dooley told them, "Don't worship any man. You are as good as me."

At the height of his spectacular medical mission in Southeast Asia he was acclaimed the seventh most admired man in America by a Gallup poll. At the same time, his mother, Peggy Dooley, was selected Woman of Achievement, an honor bestowed on "the most outstanding homemaker in the greater St. Louis area." Tom, with his characteristic humor, wired his mother: "Congratulations from number seven to number one."

Father Theodore Hesburgh, former president of Notre Dame, said of Dr. Tom: "When he first went to Southeast Asia as a young Navy medical officer in 1954, he saw with his own eyes the plight of those unfortunate people. Instead of turning away, he returned to help them with every strength he had. He was determined to serve them, his God, and his country. He became a legend in his own time."

Cardinal Francis Spellman told Dooley: "In your thirty-four years you have done what very few have done in the allotted scriptural lifetime."

President Eisenhower said, "Few men if any have equaled Dr. Dooley's exhibition of courage, self-sacrifice, faith in his God, and readiness to serve his fellowman."

Dr. Charles W. Mayo, one of those who chose Tom Dooley for a medical award, said, "Dooley was a free man helping other free men on a person-to-person basis."

At the very height of his dazzling career in 1959, Dooley discovered he had cancer. A person with less humility than Dooley may well have exploded in an emotional outburst: "Oh, God! What is wrong with you? Can't you see that I'm giving my entire life for those thousands of helpless people? I have become a legend in my own lifetime, and yet you let cancer bring to a close my work for you and your people."

It is a tribute to Tom Dooley's character that he never asked, "Why me, God?" He did not become bitter. Instead, he continued his work as best he could almost until the day he died, January 18, 1961.

Dr. Dooley told his friends that "God has given me this most hideous, painful cancer at an extremely young age for a purpose. It is a gift. He wants me to use it."

What an inspiring example! Tom Dooley did not try to unravel the mystery of suffering. He simply took it as a "gift" that God wanted him to "use."

CHAPTER FIVE

From the Trenches of World War I to Vietnam

For thirty years I had the privilege of "walking in the shadow" of the poet who wrote "Trees." From 1948 to 1978 I taught science at Campion in Prairie du Chien, Wisconsin. Joyce Kilmer loved Campion College so much that he came there as often as possible, and stayed as long as his pressing engagements would permit.

Kilmer delighted to live in the midst of the students. The intimate glimpses of the students' life thus afforded him charmed him. During his visits, Kilmer lived in the senior residence hall known as Marquette Hall. His room was next to the one I eventually lived in — the second room on the north wing of the first floor.

Every day when I walked to the classroom building to teach physics and general science, I walked under the spreading branches of the trees in front of the student chapel. Kilmer loved this elegant avenue of trees, and frequently walked there in company with his

close friend, the poet-priest Father James J.
Daly, S.J.

Joyce Kilmer began his association with
Campion on September 9, 1912. This is the date
of his first letter to Father Daly, who was at
that time professor of English literature at what
was then Campion College.

On April 27, 1916, Kilmer came to Campion
for the first time. He gave a lecture on "The War
and the Poets." He fell so much in love with
Campion that he returned in June for a week's
visit.

On April 23, 1917, seventeen days after the
United States declared war on Germany, Kilmer
volunteered for the Army. At that time, he was
just over the first draft age; and although he
was exempt from service, having a wife and four
small children, he considered it his patriotic
duty to enlist. It is said that he was influenced
in large measure by his memory of the sinking
of the *Lusitania* on May 7, 1915. The *Lusitania*,
a Cunard passenger liner, was sunk by a
German U-boat. On the occasion of the disaster,
he was asked by the editor of the *New York
Times* to write a poem for the edition of the next
day. He wrote what is considered by many one
of his best poems: "The White Ships and the
Red."

Kilmer's last visit to Campion was on June
15, 1917. At that time he was in the Army and
had to obtain military leave to come to Campion

to deliver the commencement address. This was his last formal public address. Significantly, it was entitled "The Courage of Enlightenment." He stressed the fact that in both peacetime and wartime there is a need in our country for men who have been enlightened with the proper view of the value of things, and who have the moral courage to live up to their enlightened views.

On October 31, 1917, Kilmer sailed for France. He arrived at Brest, France, almost two weeks later, on November 12. From France Kilmer wrote to his wife, Aline, "It's good for me to be a private and to be bossed around by a young snip of an officer I wouldn't hire as an office boy. Every drill night, I have about three hundred exercises in humility.

"I love you, and you are never away from me," Kilmer continued in his letter to his wife. "Pray for me that I may love God more. It seems to me that if I can learn to love God more passionately, more constantly, without distractions, that absolutely nothing else can matter."

From the trenches of World War I came Kilmer's "Poet's Prayer." It is a prayer to Christ from a tired but brave soldier:

> My shoulders ache beneath my pack,
>   Lie easier, Cross, upon His back;
> Lord, Thou didst suffer more for me,
>   Than all the hosts of land and sea;

So let me render back again,
    This millionth of Thy gift. Amen.

In April 1918, Kilmer, at his own request, was transferred to the Regimental Intelligence Section, in which service he would be up at the front, doing very important and dangerous scouting of the enemy positions. He was attached to the Second Battalion, 165th Infantry of the 42nd Division, the Rainbow Division. That same month, in recognition of his services, he was made a sergeant. In July, he was cited for bravery in a dispatch and was awarded the Croix de Guerre by a grateful French nation.

Kilmer's last day on planet earth was July 30, 1918. Since his own battalion would not be in the lead during these days, he obtained permission to advance with the First Battalion, which was under the command of then Major William J. Donovan.

Fearlessly he went out in front to reconnoiter for the position of machine-gun nests of the enemy. His final days are described by Colonel Donovan, Kilmer's former commanding officer.

> I actually knew him [Kilmer] when I was a Battalion Commander and he was with me for a few days preceding his death.
>
> He was Sergeant in the Regimental Intelligence Group. I was

ordered to make an advance. He asked to be assigned to us as the attacking battalion.

In that day's advance I watched him. I saw the way he went about his work: his earnestness, his devotion to duty, and his skill in gathering those marks and signs of the enemy which his duty required him to obtain.

That night we ran into a fight. He was part of my group. He had never been in that kind of battle before, but he very quickly fitted into the work of headquarters and did much more than his required duties.

We advanced again the next day. In that advance my Adjutant was killed beside me. I took another Lieutenant in his place. He too was killed.

In these few days I had seen the quality of Kilmer, so I pressed him into service as my Adjutant and in all the next day he did a fine job. The following afternoon we went out on a reconnaissance together. We had to crawl close to the ground. I suddenly found him missing. I went back to him, and he was dead.

I really knew him only a few days, but in those few days I learned his qualities as a soldier and as a man.

The above letter from Colonel Donovan was sent to Campion on the occasion of the dedication of the school library to Joyce Kilmer on October 31, 1937.

The Joyce Kilmer Memorial Library at Campion is said to have contained "the finest display of Kilmer mementos in the country." This included a number of his manuscripts and letters. I was delighted to find that the entire series of letters that Joyce Kilmer wrote to Father Daly was there. (Campion came to a close on August 15, 1978; the many mementos of Joyce Kilmer are now housed at Marquette University in Milwaukee.)

The one item that always fascinated me most of all was the notebook that was carried by Joyce Kilmer "at the front." In this book are the original copies of several of his poems, among them "Rouge Bouquet," and the beginning of a diary of his movements in France, while at the front.

The manuscript that claimed my special attention was the address which Joyce Kilmer gave at the Campion commencement exercises on June 15, 1917.

It was a thrill to see the copy of the citation for bravery that had been given to Joyce Kilmer. Last but not least was a pair of brass-rimmed glasses that Kilmer had to use to bring print into focus.

One of the finest tributes to Kilmer is the following poem by Joseph Bernard Rethy:

He loved the songs of nature and of art;
 He heard enchanting voices
  everywhere;
 The sight of trees against the sunlit air,
And fields of flowers, filled with joy his
  heart.

He knew the romance of the busy mart,
 The magic of Manhattan's throbbing
  life,
 And sensed the glory of the poor man's
  strife,
And humbly walked with Jesus Christ
  apart.

All kindly things were brother to his soul;
 Evil he scorned and hated every wrong;
 Gentle — another's wounds oft
  wounded him.
But when his country called the
  freedman's roll,
 Forthwith he laid aside his wondrous
  song,
 And joined in Flanders God's own
  Cherubim.

The above poem appeared in a special book published by Campion to commemorate the dedication of the Joyce Kilmer Memorial Library. The same book contains the following summary of Kilmer: "These four words, courage and self-abnegation and love and faith, are the key to Joyce Kilmer's heroic life and no less heroic death. He was a poet, a creator. A poet is one who is pursued by a love of beauty and with great things, with trees, and stars and gorgeous sunsets and sapphire seas; he was in love with little things, the ordinary things that seem so humdrum to the rest of us who are not poets, and out of that love he created with the witchery of words poems about bookshops, and railroad trains, and alarm clocks and delicatessen shops — all transmuted by the magic of his imagination into things of glory.

"He was in love with humanity in all its phases, and, as a consequence, we have an unforgettable picture of servant girls and grocer boys, his friends, his children, and his beloved wife who inspired some of his loveliest poems. Most of all he was in love with God and the things of God."

In Joyce Kilmer we have the inspiring example of a man of letters who volunteered to give his life for his country. He died with a bullet through his brain. Kilmer is acclaimed as the only poet of established reputation who fell fighting in World War I. It is noteworthy that during World War I many young poets voluntarily entered the various military branches and fought among the ranks of the Allies.

World War II brought us heroes of still

another kind — civilians who were caught up in the cancer of Nazi madness that crept across Europe. It was a madness that brought death to millions and terrorized anyone who dared to care. Let us now look at the life of one of those who cared.

In Haarlem, Holland, a devout Christian woman by the name of Corrie ten Boom spent the first fifty years of her life quietly in her home in the Netherlands. The daughter of a watchmaker, she lived happily with her father and sister in their small home over their shop. She became a watchmaker herself.

When the Nazi invaders stomped across the border into Holland, the ten Boom family joined the underground movement to help Jews escape the country. As soon as the Nazis forged a ring of steel around Holland, however, the Jews were no longer able to escape.

Unable to stand by and watch the horror of persecution that went on around them, the ten Boom family became daring resistance fighters. They furnished an ingenious "hiding place" for Jewish refugees under threat of imprisonment.

In February 1944, the ten Boom family was betrayed. Booted Nazis stormed through the door of their shop. The ten Boom family and their friends were rounded up at gunpoint and herded into trucks and freight cars. Their destination — the concentration camps.

For the next ten months Corrie lived in a

nightmare. She endured four months of solitary confinement. She was transported to the female extermination camp in Ravensbruck, Germany. Here she watched her fellow prisoners disappear into the camp crematorium. Each day she expected that she too would be sent into the crematorium.

During the long months of her imprisonment in a series of brutal concentration camps, Corrie was able to communicate by letter with friends in the outside world. These letters, miraculously saved from destruction even in the tumult of war, give us an insight into the nobility of her soul.

When Corrie heard that her father had died, she rejoiced. Yes, *rejoiced* — because his death meant that he was no longer a prisoner in the Nazi concentration camp. He had escaped from the sufferings of this life. He had entered into his life of joy and glory.

"How happy he is now," Corrie wrote, "for he sees the answer to everything." For her beloved father, suffering was no longer a mystery. How wonderful it will be for us also when, on one happy day in our heavenly home, we too shall understand the *why* of suffering.

The one thing that caused Corrie the greatest pain was to be forced to witness the brutality of the guards toward her fellow prisoners, especially toward her ailing sister,

Betsie. With a feeling of utter helplessness Corrie watched Betsie die.

"The worst for us is not that which we suffer ourselves but the suffering which we see around us." These words of Corrie ten Boom echo the sentiments of each of us when we are forced by circumstances to watch helplessly while our dear loved ones suffer.

Corrie's prayer of acceptance and resignation is inspirational: "We are also learning to put the worst in the hands of the Savior. When all the securities of the world are falling away, then you realize, like never before, what it means to have your security in Jesus."

Just before she died, Betsie told her sister, Corrie, "Only prisoners can know how desperate this life is. We can tell from experience that no pit is too deep, because God's everlasting arms always sustain us."

Through an almost miraculous release, Corrie ten Boom was set free just one week before all women her age in the Ravensbruck prison were to be put to death.

The incredible account of the ten Boom family's resistance to Nazi cruelty and the horrors of the concentration camps were brought home to millions in an all-time best-selling book, *The Hiding Place*.

When this book was made into a motion picture, the impact was even more overpowering. In graphic detail that was at times frightening, the film brought out the enormity of the Nazi evil. Some of the comments voiced were:

- I found this film both depressing, and inspirational.
- It was depressing to witness at Ravensbruck "man's inhumanity to man."
- It was inspiring to see the remarkable courage of Corrie ten Boom.

A most trying circumstance came to Corrie after the war. She encountered a nurse who had treated her sister brutally at Ravensbruck. Corrie wrote of this meeting: "When I saw her, a feeling of bitterness, almost hatred, came into my heart. How my dying sister had suffered because of her. I knew I had to forgive her, but I could not."

Corrie met this problem the same way she had met other dilemmas and problems at Ravensbruck. She prayed to God for guidance and forgiveness. Corrie did more than forgive the nurse. She converted her to Christ!

At approximately the same time that the ten Boom family made their Haarlem, Holland, home a "hiding place" for Jewish refugees, another incredible chapter in human suffering and patience was being written in Amsterdam.

In order to escape destruction at the hands of the Nazis, a group of Jews took to hiding in the attic of an old warehouse. The youngest member of the group was Anne Frank, a thirteen-year-old who kept a diary during those long months of hiding in the "Secret Annexe," as she called their hideaway.

Anne Frank's *Diary of a Young Girl* is a story of bravery and love. Anne was like all girls her age, passing through the heights and depths of growing-up years. Here is a story of faith and struggle, of love and friendship, of the inside and the outside of the human heart. One thing that gave the Frank family courage during the long months of hiding was their faith in God. It was a faith that could cry out with the psalmist, "I lift up my eyes to the mountains. My help is in the name of the Lord" (see Psalm 121:1).

"We must be brave and strong and accept all inconveniences and not grumble, must do what is within our power and trust in God," wrote Anne.

I never appreciated the full impact of the above words until I saw the play *The Diary of Anne Frank* presented by Duchesne Academy in Omaha, Nebraska. I was overwhelmed to realize that some dozen people were crowded together in a dirty old attic with a leaky roof and broken windows. The occupants must have felt like sardines in a can or like animals in cages.

Time and again in her diary Anne mentions how she would like to take a walk in spring and watch the green grass beginning to grow, and then look at the buds breaking forth on the branches of the trees. Alas, she dare not leave her attic prison. Its dirty walls and sagging roof marked the limits of her universe for long, long months.

Despite the unending monotony and the dwindling supply of food, Anne did not falter in her trust in God. She continued to say her long evening prayers "earnestly."

In her diary entry for Friday, March 31, 1944, Anne wrote, "God has not left me alone, and will not leave me alone."

By her example Anne gave proof to the words of a poet, "Regardless of circumstances, each person lives in a world of his own making." Anne's "world" was that of books and literature. She read wide and wisely. To her diary Anne confided her dream of the future: After the British and Americans would crush the Nazi invasion, and she could once again return to normal life, Anne hoped to become an author.

In the entry dated Tuesday, April 4, 1944, Anne wrote, "I am grateful to God for giving me this gift of writing, of expressing all that is in me. I can shake off everything if I write; my sorrow disappears, my courage is reborn. I can recapture everything when I write, my thoughts, my ideals, and my fantasies."

Four months after Anne wrote the above lines proved to be the most dreadful day in Anne's life. On August 4, 1944, the Grune Polizei made a raid on the "Secret Annexe." All the occupants were arrested and sent to concentration camps. In March of 1945, two months before the liberation of Holland, Anne died in the concentration camp at Bergen-Belsen.

Anne's mother died at Auschwitz on January 6, 1945. Her father, Otto Frank, survived to be liberated by the Russians. In May 1945 the war ended. Several months later Otto Frank returned to Amsterdam.

When the Gestapo had plundered the "Secret Annexe" in August of 1944, they left scattered on the floor a pile of books, magazines, and newspapers. Buried in this pile was Anne's diary. Friends of the family later rescued this diary and presented it to Otto Frank upon his return to Amsterdam. Otto had copies of the diary privately circulated as a memorial to his family. It was a Dutch university professor who urged formal publication of the book, which became a best-seller, and was translated into thirty-one languages.

The agony that Anne Frank endured during World War II was long and drawn out. By contrast, the disaster that Max Cleland suffered in Vietnam took place in a flash.

One morning when the sun came up in Vietnam, Max Cleland was a vigorous combat soldier. Then, in a split second of time, a grenade blew away his legs and one arm. Following the loss of three of his limbs, Max

Cleland sank into a swamp of despair so deep and dark he thought for a time that he would never be able to struggle out of it.

The first step to recovery, Max found out, was terribly difficult. It was to accept the suffering that had come his way. During the endless days he was stretched out on a hospital bed in Vietnam, Max kept replaying the grenade explosion like a videotape in his memory. If only he could have changed the sequence of events on that dreadful day. But, no matter how hard he tried, he was forced back to reality. He was a disabled veteran.

Help finally came to Max when he realized the truth in the serenity prayer: "God, grant me the serenity to accept the things I cannot change, courage to change the things I can, and wisdom to know the difference."

About this time Max recalled the words of Alexander Graham Bell, the great inventor, who gave us the telephone: "When one door closes, another opens, but we often look so long and so regretfully upon the closed door that we do not see the one that has opened for us."

And this is when Max began to ask himself what he had left. "I still had my mind," the disabled veteran concluded. "I still had the intelligence God had given me. I still had one good arm that could propel a wheelchair. I could still travel from place to place."

The third important lesson took Max many

years to learn. After serving two terms as a state senator in Georgia, Max decided to run for lieutenant governor. He banked everything on it, and lost.

Max was crushed. Once again he found himself sinking into a quagmire of self-pity and deep depression. Some months later, while he was driving in the rain up to Washington to take a U.S. Senate staff position, he suddenly realized that he could go no farther by himself. There, on that rain-swept highway he cried out, "God, help me! God, forgive me!"

Max went on to say that God did indeed come to him. Max found more meaning, more purpose, and more joy in life than he ever had thought possible.

Nine years after the grenade explosion in Vietnam that cost him both legs and one arm, Max Cleland was appointed in 1977 to head the Veterans Administration in Washington, D.C.

"Here are three bits of advice," says Max, "that I'd like to offer to anyone who is faced with some crushing burden or handicap. Strive for acceptance. Look for an open door. Let God help you."

The following prayer has become identified with Max Cleland. He closes many of his speeches and interviews with it. The origin of the prayer is unknown, although it is believed to have been written by a Confederate soldier during the Civil War.

I asked God for strength, that I might
    achieve,
I was made weak, that I might learn
    humbly to obey.
I asked for health, that I might do greater
    things,
I was given infirmity, that I might do
    better things.
I asked for riches, that I might be happy,
I was given poverty, that I might be wise.
I asked for power, that I might have the
    praise of men,
I was given weakness, that I might feel
    the need of God.
I asked for all things, that I might enjoy
    life,
I was given life, that I might enjoy all
    things.
I got nothing that I asked for — but
    everything I had hoped for.
Almost despite myself, my unspoken
    prayers were answered.
I am, among all men, most richly blessed.

CHAPTER SIX

Gallant Women

A few years after World War II, I
had the privilege of meeting Maria
von Trapp and her singing family
when they came to Prairie du Chien, Wisconsin.
Their program of beautiful, inspiring music was
given on the campus of Campion High School,
where I was teaching physics at the time.

Baroness Maria von Trapp is the heroine of
one of the most famous motion pictures of all
times, *The Sound of Music*. This spectacular
film showed how the Trapp family fled Austria
in the early days of the Nazi occupation.

When the Trapp family left Austria during
the time of Hitler, everything they owned was
left behind. After a few singing engagements in
Europe they came to America with nothing
except their skill to sing together as a family
and the promise of a few engagements. Their
singing was well received all across the United
States.

The Trapps traveled up into the Green
Mountains of Vermont and found an area that

reminded them of their native country. They purchased the land and built a home on a hillside overlooking the village of Stowe, Vermont. As friends came to visit, the Trapps added to their home to accommodate the ever-increasing number of visitors. Wings were added to the home and the slow evolution of a true Austrian home and lodge took place.

A few days before Christmas, 1980, the Trapp family home caught fire in the early hours of the morning and went up in smoke. Maria's son, Johannes, assisted her from the lodge apartment where she lived. Maria and her son stood in sub-zero cold watching the flames leap sixty feet into the sky. By midday only the blackened chimneys remained, pointing their fingers upward through the rubble of what had been one of the most colorful lodges in the area.

Everything that Maria had accumulated over the previous forty years in America and in her travels around the world was destroyed. "Losing money is no comparison," said Maria. "What I lost was irreplaceable."

As mother and son watched the fire consume the building, words of faith formed on Maria's lips. Not bitterness toward life, not anger toward God, but words of acceptance: "The Lord has given, the Lord takes away, blessed be the name of the Lord."

Maria then turned to her son, and said, "You have always complained our house was not built correctly for a lodge. Now you will have the chance to build it perfectly."

To those who might experience tragedy or loss of irreplaceable possessions, Maria von Trapp says, "We would like to advise God how to arrange our lives. What things will happen, and what will not. He has a purpose in everything, but we don't always understand. Remember that God knows what he is doing, and he has a purpose. It must turn out all right."

Born about the same time as Baroness Maria von Trapp, but on this side of the Atlantic, was a woman who became author, editor, playwright, foreign correspondent, and ambassador. Clare Boothe Luce, who died in October of 1987, was still in her twenties when she became associate editor of *Vogue* magazine in 1930. The next year she was named to a similar position with *Vanity Fair* magazine, of which she became managing editor in 1933. That same year she wrote *Stuffed Shirts*, the first of her three books. In 1937 she wrote *Abide with Me*, the first of seven plays.

In 1943, she was elected to the U.S. House of Representatives from Connecticut. She became an influential member of the House military affairs committee. In 1953, she was called by President Dwight Eisenhower to serve as ambassador to Italy, a post she held until 1957. In that year, she was awarded the Laetare Medal by the University of Notre Dame.

In 1946, Mrs. Luce's daughter, Ann, a student at Stanford University, was killed in a car accident. That same year, after the accident, Clare Boothe Luce was received into the Church by Bishop Fulton Sheen. Another great influence was the famed Father John Courtney Murray, S.J. Mrs. Luce is not hesitant to point out that it was her newly found faith that helped her come to terms with the suffering caused by the loss of her daughter.

"When Ann died," said Mrs. Luce, "I received many letters of sympathy. Often they came from women who had lost their only daughter in some tragic way too. 'Why should such a thing happen to me and to you?' they asked. 'What have we done to deserve this? It's not fair.' And at first this was my own thought as well. I couldn't understand why Ann had to die so young and why I had to give her up."

Clare Boothe Luce reminds us, "We don't understand pain and suffering. We know that they come unfailing, but we still don't consent to give them a place in our life."

Mrs. Luce mentioned that her faith didn't change her life-style. What it changed was her outlook. It gave meaning to everything. "Faith is the difference between the freezing cold and sunshine — or shivering in a cold house and having someone turn on the heat. Faith is light and warmth. It has made my life meaningful. It gave me the strength and courage to go on.

Knowing and realizing God's love for me changed my attitude toward everything that was going on within me and around me."

Maria von Trapp twice in her lifetime lost her home and all material possessions. Clare Boothe Luce lost her daughter, Ann. No woman in the public gaze, however, whom I know, has suffered as many losses and tragedies as Mrs. Rose Kennedy: the retardation of her daughter Rosemary; the assassinations of Jack and Bobby; the death of Joe, Jr., in action during World War II; the death of Kathleen in an air crash; Ted's severe injuries in a plane crash, and then his involvement in the Mary Jo Kopechne drowning; the paralysis of her husband following a severe stroke, and his ultimate death.

Time and again Mrs. Kennedy has been asked, "How can you go on in the face of all the tragedy that has befallen you?"

Mrs. Kennedy admits that her answer does not satisfy everyone. "I believe it is a matter of will — God's will and my will. Early in life I decided that I would not be overcome by events. My philosophy has been that, regardless of the circumstances, I shall not be vanquished, but will try to be happy. Life is not easy for any of us. But it is a continual challenge, and it is up to us to be cheerful — and to be strong, so that those who depend on us may draw strength from our example."

Rose Kennedy informs us that in sorrow we must look outward, rather than inward, and thus secure peace of mind. Her philosophy is simple and straightforward: "I believe in keeping interested, growing, and learning."

The most important element of all, according to Rose, is faith. She admits that many times in her life she was comforted by the magnificent *Meditation* written in the nineteenth century by Cardinal John Henry Newman, the famous English churchman and author: "God has created me to do Him some definite service. I am a link in a chain, a bond of connection between persons. He has not created me for naught. I shall do good. If I am in sickness, my sickness may serve Him. If I am in sorrow, my sorrow may serve Him. He does nothing in vain. He may take away my friends. He may throw me among strangers. He may make me feel desolate, make my spirit sick, hide my future from me — still He knows what He is about."

So far in this chapter we have considered how mature women have met the tragedies that swept across their lives. Pain and suffering, however, affect the young as well as those older.

It took a fraction of time on a hot July day in 1967 to totally change the course of Joni Eareckson's young life. In those few seconds, her past became nothing more than a collection of distant memories. Her future became broken promises and shattered dreams. Her present became a nightmare.

Joni Eareckson was voted the "most outstanding girl athlete" in her high-school class. Only a month after graduation, a tragic diving accident left her paralyzed from the neck down. In a split second she lost the promise of that bright beginning and was handed a future of tears and despair.

During her first months in the hospital, she was so helpless that she could not even do what she longed to do — take her own life. She begged a girl friend to do it for her several times, but the friend refused.

Encased in a canvas Stryker frame, Eareckson felt life was meaningless. All those yardsticks for success that had come to mean so much to her were shattered — being pretty and popular, dating the right guys. After waves of depression and a phase of reading the works of existentialists and atheists, Joni gradually came back to a deepened version of her Christian faith.

During the long and grueling months of tough rehabilitation, Joni taught herself to draw and paint, holding a pen or a brush between her teeth. Then came speaking tours and writing, in which she used her own faith to encourage the despairing and disabled.

In 1979, Joni organized a national "ministry to those who suffer" called "Joni and Friends."

She began to tell the story of her joyous, newfound faith in Christ, first to small groups, then to people across the country, on television talk shows, in *Guideposts* magazine, and on a Billy Graham Crusade telecast.

Her inspiring life story, *Joni*, became an all-time best-seller, with over two million copies in print. This book was made into a motion picture in which Joni beautifully and skillfully portrays herself. Released in 1980, this inspiring film won immediate and wide acclaim.

Joni faces head-on the universal problem that is central to her life and as old as the book of Job. If a loving God exists, why do the good and innocent suffer? With utter honesty Joni admits, "If God's mind was small enough for me to understand, he wouldn't be God."

In addition to her autobiography, *Joni*, which appeared in 1976, Joni wrote a second book entitled *A Step Further*, published in 1978. Her two books have sold more than four million copies.

Joni concludes that man cannot understand the whys and ways of God regarding pain, but that knowledge of Christ's life and suffering makes pain endurable. "Sometimes," confesses Joni, "I can't stand being in a wheelchair, but then God's grace takes over. Even in my handicap God has a plan and purpose for my life."

The one thing that gives Joni the most

comfort and reassurance is the fact that we are Easter people and heaven is our home. On one happy day in our future we shall have our own personal resurrection. In heaven each of us shall have our own glorified body.

"The good things here," says Joni, "are merely miniatures of the better things we will know in heaven. It's like the artwork I produce. I draw scenes from nature around me, but those drawings are only a feeble, sketchy attempt to mirror what I see. I imitate with a gray pencil what God has painted with an infinite array of colors."

Each of the four women mentioned so far in this chapter brought us her message of joy and beauty by different means. Maria von Trapp sang songs of love and courage. Clare Boothe Luce wrote books and plays. Rose Kennedy showed us strength of character and perseverance in the face of many personal tragedies. Joni Eareckson relayed her message via motion pictures, TV appearances, and lovely drawings.

The last woman we will consider in this chapter is Helen Steiner Rice. She has been called "the most popular Christian poet in the modern world." Thousands of people regularly buy and exchange the sensitive greeting cards she has written. In churches and homes across the country her reverent words are used to add meaning to sermons, Sunday school lessons, and family devotions.

In addition to her poems that appear on greeting cards, she has written half a dozen books of inspirational poetry. No wonder Helen Steiner Rice has been called "America's favorite inspirational poet." Few people have been able to express their faith in such clear, simple, beautiful words. And few people have reached so many with words that inspire, words that comfort, words that bring hope. Her clear and direct style and the invincible faith that shines from every line make her poems both unforgettable and spirit-lifting for readers of all ages.

Mrs. Rice has known sorrow and heartbreak in her own life, and her faith has seen her through each trial. Most of all she has inspired her friends with the shining example of a steadfast faith that did not falter even in the face of a long and debilitating illness. The Lord, for whom she had labored so long, called her home on April 23, 1981, at the age of seventy-nine.

As we read the poems of Helen Steiner Rice we all feel instinctively that we are close to her in a very personal way . . . but we still want to know her better. There are so many fascinating details we want to fill in about her life.

In the October 1976 issue of *Guideposts* magazine, Mrs. Rice gives us the following insight into her character. She prefaces the article with this statement: "Every time a tragedy entered my life, God showed me it was not a dead end, but only a detour."

She continues: "Twice in my lifetime I thought my world had come to an end. I thought that all meaning and purpose were gone and that there was no reason to go on living. Yet, in both cases, what I did not know was that God had something excitingly new in store for me, that He would actually use those devastating personal losses to lift my soul into new spiritual consciousness and lead my life into new areas of service I never would have dreamed possible.

"Of course I couldn't see any good in either of those heartbreaking experiences at the time. We never can. But now, with the luxury of a full life's experiences behind me, I am no longer looking at the back side of the tapestry, and I see much more clearly how all sorts of adversity — defeat, loneliness, disappointment, rejection, illness — can be used as a springboard to spiritual triumph.

"The bitterest pills I've had to swallow both deal with the death of loved ones. The first came when I was 16 and a senior in high school. It was doubly traumatic, first because it came so suddenly and second because it was set against the backdrop of an unbelievably secure and happy childhood.

"I grew up in Lorain, Ohio, a bustling steel

town on the shores of Lake Erie. My dad was a railroad engineer for the Baltimore and Ohio, which was a good job, but not so good that it elevated us above our neighbors. Dad was a warm, gentle man with an amazingly wide sphere of friends.

"Mother was a dedicated homemaker and gifted seamstress. Mother, my sister, and I were usually candidates for the fashion magazines when we strolled Reid Avenue on our way to 20th Street Methodist Church each Sunday.

"Then, suddenly, in the fall of 1918, Dad became ill. A flu epidemic was sweeping the country, taking many lives. In a matter of days, he was gone, another flu victim.

"The great emptiness I felt the night of his death still causes something to stir inside me. I was so young, so vulnerable, so unaccepting. Standing on the back porch of our Reid Avenue house that cold, windy October night, I can remember sobbing over and over, 'Why? Why, God?'

"Instead of going off to Ohio Wesleyan to study law as I'd planned, I went to work. Though we were not destitute, I wanted to stay close to home to help. My job was with the Ohio Public Service Company, doing an odd assortment of assignments at first, until I was asked to become public relations director.

"I really worked hard learning everything I could about the company, determined to know the electric-power business inside and out. I also became active in the National Electric Light Association and was named chairman of its women's committee on public relations.

"One speech I'll never forget was one made to the American Electric Railways Convention in Washington. After my talk, I had my picture taken with President Coolidge and received the praise of B.C. Forbes, publisher of *Forbes Magazine*. He said I should leave Lorain and come to New York where 'there is so much more room for doing big things.'

"Though I didn't move my base of operations, I did form my own lecture bureau, and my speaking assignments increased. One took me to Dayton in 1928 to address a group of bankers. Afterward, a handsome young man named Franklin D. Rice, an officer with Dayton Savings and Trust, invited me to have dinner with him. I found him a wonderful person, warm and sensitive. We saw a lot of each other and within a year we were married.

"The wedding was conducted by the Rev. Daniel Poling, in New York City's historic Marble Collegiate Church. Franklin was a prominent businessman, intelligent and wealthy. We honeymooned on a ship in the Caribbean and returned to a big house with Tiffany chandeliers and servants to polish them. And for my wedding present, Franklin gave me a watch surrounded by 100 diamonds. It was one big make-believe ball, but, like Cinderella's, it was not to last.

"Much of my husband's wealth was invested in stocks. During the Great Depression, when the market crashed, he lost heavily. However, he did what wise investors do in bad times — he bought more. After all, he reasoned, the prices would look cheap when the market rebounded. But, of course, it didn't rebound — not until much, much later. Finally everything we owned was gone, and, without any warning, so was Franklin. He had broken from the strain. A note he left me read, 'Darling, the only thing I'm sorry about is that I never could give you all the things I meant to. You'll always go on. I only knew one world. I just can't become a bum — I have to go out with the band playing.'

"It was like the shock that came with my father's death. I had no idea what I would do, if in fact I wanted to do anything. Then, out of the blue, the Gibson Greeting Card Company in Cincinnati asked me to come to work for them. 'Make a survey of our cards and tell us how to improve them,' the officers instructed me. I did as they said and came back with hundreds of recommendations. They accepted most of them, implemented them, and when the editor's job became vacant I was appointed to fill it. That was in 1934.

"For several years I edited the company's cards, but did little writing. I did create my own little greetings for friends, writing a verse on some special occasion, but those messages were not salable. According to the experts, my thoughts were too sentimental, too religious. In the 1950s, though, Gibson did publish some of my verses, offering them in a few markets with modest results.

"Many people wrote me, however, and the spiritual help they received from the things I wrote greatly encouraged me. The response of people has always been my greatest reward. Then, in 1960, a performer named Aladdin read a verse I'd written called 'The Priceless Gift of Christmas' on the Lawrence Welk Show. The response of the public was overwhelming. Thousands of people wrote to ask where they could find other poems like that one.

"Since then, God has opened a whole new world of friends to me. The simple verses I've written have been reproduced by the millions. They have been read on network TV, appeared in thousands of periodicals, in dozens of books.

"All I do is put down the words God places on my heart, and then He does the rest. He even finds the people who need to hear them. I'm the world's worst promoter of my verses. I leave the distribution of the words I put on paper to the Author, the One who inspires them.

" 'So where do you go from here?' someone asked recently, knowing full well that I'm already beyond three score and ten in years. My answer is, 'One day at a time, as He directs.' I know that at my age, time is getting short, but I've faced what I thought was the end of the road before, and each time I've discovered what I wrote in this poem:

> "When we feel we have nothing left to
>   give,
> And we are sure that the song has ended,
> When our day seems over and the
>   shadows fall,
> And the darkness of night has descended,
> Where can we go to find the strength to
>   valiantly keep on trying?
> Where can we find the hand that will dry
>   the tears that the heart is crying?
> There's but one place to go and that is to
>   God
> And, dropping all pretense and pride,
> We can pour out our problems without
>   restraint,
> And gain strength with Him at our side.
> And together we stand at life's
>   crossroads,
> And view what we think is the end,
> But God has a much bigger vision
> And He tells us it's only a bend,
> For the road goes on and is smoother,
> And the pause in the song is a rest,
> And the part that's unsung and
>   unfinished

Is the sweetest and richest and best.
So rest and relax and grow stronger,
Let go and let God share your load,
Your work is not finished or ended,
You've just come to a bend in the road."

During the summer of 1976, Mrs. Rice was confined for three months in a Cincinnati hospital with a very complicated back problem that completely limited her physically. With utter honesty she admitted, "I wish I could write to you and tell you I am now sitting on top of the world and filled with renewed enthusiasm and endless zip, zeal, and zing, but this has been a very difficult period in my life, and it presents unbelievable problems. But I am certainly accepting this as one of the greatest gifts God ever sent to me."

Over the years, I have written to Helen Steiner Rice for permission to make use of her lovely poems in my books and various other publications. Mrs. Rice was always most kind and gracious in giving me permission to make use of her poems. She once said, "If you were touched by the beauty you found in some word or line, it was *your soul's reflection* in *proximity* with *mine!*"

In the last years of her life, Mrs. Rice was unable to write to me personally, so her secretary, Mary Jo Eling, was most cooperative in relaying permissions to me.

I would like to share with you now my favorite poem from the pen of Helen Steiner Rice, entitled "My God Is No Stranger":

I've never seen God,
   but I know how I feel. . .
It's people like you
   who make Him "so real". . .
My God is no stranger,
   He's friendly and gay. . .
And He doesn't ask me
   to weep when I pray. . .
It seems that I pass Him
   so often each day. . .
In the faces of people
   I meet on my way. . .
He's the stars in the heaven,
   a smile on some face,
A leaf on a tree
   or a rose in a vase. . .
He's winter and autumn
   and summer and spring. . .
In short, God is Every
   Real, Wonderful Thing. . .
I wish I might meet Him
   much more than I do. . .
I would if there were
   more people like you.

One of the most treasured experiences of my life took place on the evening of October 15, 1982, at the "Archbishop's Educational

Development Dinner" in the Red Lion Inn in Omaha, Nebraska. The main speaker was Mrs. Robert (Dolores) Hope. After the dinner I had the unique good luck of talking with Mrs. Hope and her son, Kelly.

During her inspiring talk during the dinner, and in her informal conversation with people afterward, Dolores Hope dwelled on such topics as marriage, loneliness, motherhood, and education.

A middle-aged woman asked Dolores to explain her secret — how she and Bob had managed to have forty-eight years of married life, while Hollywood stars all around them were turning marriage into a game of musical chairs.

With utter directness, Dolores replied that she obtained great strength from her Catholic religion. To her, Christ was not a mere historical figure; he is a friend whose footsteps move in rhythm with her own.

A young woman then questioned Dolores about the lonely Christmas seasons she must have experienced while her husband was entertaining our troops overseas. (According to news releases, Bob Hope has performed for more than two million GIs. Since 1941, he has amassed a staggering record of over six million miles of travel by air.)

Dolores admitted that there were times when she was lonely while her world-famous husband was on the other side of planet earth, yet she minimized her own loneliness.

She said that it puzzled her during wartime — World War II, Korea, Vietnam — that so many people showed her so much sympathy because Bob was away at Christmas. She thought of the wives of men in the U.S. armed forces who were gone for years. She pointed out that wives of professionals such as doctors, as well as the spouses of those in the military, frequently face loneliness also.

Dolores is a realist who faces the fact that life makes each person walk alone on many occasions. The state of being alone is inevitable. Each person, even if he loves and is loved very deeply, must meet his quota of moments alone.

Mrs. Hope went on to say, "You should look at the world the way it really is. You'll find some sadness and some disappointments, but I don't think you'll find the confusion and despair that the communications media seem to present. I like being with people, but I also need to have my time alone."

The next person to question Dolores was a well-dressed young woman who looked like an executive from an advertising firm on Madison Avenue. "Didn't you have regrets about giving up your singing career and staying home to become a housewife and mother?"

With a sparkle in her eyes and joy in her voice, Dolores responded: "I have no regrets about that. I never felt deprived, being a housewife and mother. I thought it was great. Naturally there were times when it was a little bit dull, a little tiring. But that's normal."

Dolores emphasized the importance of a mother in the training and education of her children. There is no one closer to a child than its mother. Of course children also need their fathers — the family structure is very important. But Mother is essential.

Mother's belief in the worth and the possibilities of her child qualifies her as the educator par excellence. The home is the child's first classroom. Here, in an atmosphere of love and understanding, a child should be molded in body and mind into the type of citizen who will be a credit to the nation. The home is the first laboratory for good citizenship. It is the basic unit in our society. It should be the medium for teaching ideals of conduct that will make its future citizens law-abiding and responsible.

By her own choice, Dolores Hope remained a private figure while her husband was becoming the world's most celebrated entertainer. With Bob away so much of the time, Dolores did not waste time feeling lonely. Without fanfare she pursued her own activities as board chairman of the Eisenhower Medical Center in Rancho Mirage, California, and as a member of the boards of directors of Mutual of Omaha, the John F. Kennedy Center for the

Performing Arts in Washington, D.C., and House Ear Institute of Los Angeles.

Dolores has received several awards, including the first Gift of Life Award presented by the Holy Family Adoption Services in Los Angeles and the Red Jacket Award "for service to the community, state, and country." Mrs. Hope was named Woman of the Year by the *Los Angeles Times* in 1971.

She has served as honorary mayor of Palm Desert, California, for a number of years, and is also active in the Performing Arts Council of the Los Angeles Music Center, which she and Bob founded.

Now that her children are grown up, Dolores accompanies her husband on many of his trips visiting the sick and injured in the United States and foreign countries.

One such visit was to the Madonna Rehabilitation Center in Fremont, Nebraska. My brother-in-law was a patient there at the time, and he spoke with glowing enthusiasm of the impression that Dolores and Bob had on the entire hospital, the patients, staff, and everyone they met. The one thing that impressed people most of all was the fact that Dolores and Bob took such a personal interest in everyone they met.

In addition to her many official duties, Dolores Hope pursues a number of hobbies. Her number-one hobby is golf. In fact, golf has become so all-consuming it has become a way of life. Dolores also loves to play the piano, and do needlepoint. A domestic hobby in which Dolores excels is cooking. Italian food is her specialty. Among her close friends she is known for her antipasto salad.

Dolores admires her husband's unflagging energy, his optimism, his ability to find humor in every situation, admitting, "My husband is a good deal more patient than I am, more understanding of people and situations. He's the one who taught me a lot about accepting things the way they are, not the way you'd like to have them. That has helped me to have a happier life."

Perhaps we can profit from Dolores Hope's words and remind ourselves when things don't seem to be going our way that we are more likely to lead happier and more satisfied lives by being more accepting of the way things are.

CHAPTER SEVEN

Stouthearted Men

In his most timely, dynamic, and very important book *The Hundredth Monkey*, the gifted author Ken Keyes, Jr., informs us, "We don't live in isolation. We are all interconnected. We all live in one world. It's time we begin to realize that you and I are far more alike than we are different. We are all fellow beings traveling the road of life together."

Since we are far more alike than different, it will help us in our journey through life if we stop and consider how some of our fellow human beings have met pain and suffering with patience and endurance.

When I recall the life of the late Hubert H. Humphrey, the distinguished senator from Minnesota, I begin to believe that for some of us life may be compared to a gusty symphony set to every key and tempo. There are brief passages of ineffable tenderness, momentary measures of hope, drably padded intervals of maneuvering and modulation, spiced with

---

occasional breathtaking crescendos that rip shrilly up the chromatic scale.

H.H. Humphrey said that when he was a boy growing up on the plains of South Dakota, his father taught him that adversity is part of daily life. All too vividly Hubert recalled the searing heat of summer, the dust storms, and the longs years of drought. In January, the wolf of winter ran like a fury through the naked fields; snarling, he sniffed around the barn and house, a starveling gaunt, mean, and grim.

One of Hubert's saddest memories is that of his mother crying and his dad with tears in his eyes because they had to sell their home to pay their bills.

Hubert said that the worst moment in his life was when he discovered that he had cancer. There were days when he became discouraged. Because of the chemotherapy he lost a lot of hair and got much thinner. His pants no longer fit. His shirt collar became the wrong size.

During the time he was taking X-ray treatments, Hubert had to get up in the middle of the night with bladder spasms, saying, "I was in such agony, I honestly wanted to give it all up. But even in the deepest despair you have to look up — keep your eyes on the mountaintop." Humphrey admitted that there is no answer to the question "How long should a person live?"

What is important is how we live, and what we live for. Our lives are not in our own hands, but in the hands of God. The biggest mistake people make is giving up. Adversity is an experience, not a final act. Some people look upon any setback as the end. They're always looking for the benediction rather than the invocation.

With outspoken honesty Hubert admitted, "Like anybody else's, my faith is sometimes rocked. When I'm feeling low, I draw strength from the prayer of St. Francis of Assisi. I think it is the perfect prayer."

This is the prayer attributed to St. Francis, generally known as the "Prayer for Peace":

> Lord, make me an instrument of your
>   peace.
> Where there is hatred, let me sow love;
> where there is injury, pardon;
> where there is discord, unity;
> where there is doubt, faith;
> where there is despair, hope;
> where there is darkness, light;
> where there is sadness, joy.
> O Divine Master,
> grant that I may not so much seek to be
>   consoled, as to console;
> to be understood, as to understand;
> to be loved, as to love.
> For it is in giving, that we receive;
> it is in pardoning, that we are pardoned;

and it is in dying, that we are born to eternal life. Amen.

In Hubert H. Humphrey we had a representative from the world of politics. Our next representative is from the world of business.

Mr. Emmett J. Culligan was the founder of Culligan Soft Water Service, which is worldwide and, at this writing, distributing good water to fifty-five nations of the world. After World War I, Emmett Joseph Culligan became interested in water conditioning, and spent the following forty-four years helping establish this new industry. His fertile imagination resulted in inventions that are the foundation for a great new public utility which he founded and which carries his name.

Chemical Engineering magazine said of him: "Culligan is the greatest name in water."

Emmett Culligan created a new way of life for thousands, who daily bring the benefits of conditioned water to millions, not only in America, but around the world. He started a revolution in a great cause — that of giving pure conditioned water to mankind.

Today, in the Culligan system, there are upwards of ten thousand heads of families employed, delivering over fifty billion gallons of conditioned water to several million homes.

In 1949, in recognition of Mr. Culligan's

charity and his Christian concern for his fellowmen, Pope Pius XII conferred upon him the Knighthood of the Order of St. Gregory the Great. In 1961, the founder of Culligan Soft Water Service was made a Knight of Malta.

In March 1969, over five hundred schools and colleges across the nation chose Mr. Culligan as one of ten outstanding Americans whose lives are an inspiration to youth.

In his letter to Mr. Culligan, announcing the results of the nationwide poll, Dr. Kenneth John Beebe, president of the Horatio Alger Awards Committee of the American Schools and Colleges Association, said, "Your life is an inspiring demonstration of our country as a land of opportunity for those whose courage and faith triumphed over obstacles."

My first meeting with Mr. Culligan took place in an interesting manner. During June and July of 1966, at the request of the National Science Foundation, I was conducting a summer institute in physics for elementary-school personnel at Creighton University in Omaha, Nebraska. One afternoon I received a letter from Mr. Culligan saying that through a bit of good luck he had come across my textbook *Adventures in Science*. This book convinced him that I was the one who could write a book for him on the subject of water. He offered to pay all my expenses if I would come to his home in

San Bernardino, California, where he would outline for me the plans he had for the book.

Immediately after summer school was over, I headed west. On Wednesday afternoon, August 10, 1966, I had the golden opportunity of meeting Mr. Culligan and his wife, Anna.

Emmett's smile was as warm as the California sun and his embrace as expansive as that of Pope John's. His eyes twinkled with Irish humor. His speech was like sunlight on the heather.

Religion to Mr. Culligan was not something you put on like a coat on Sunday to go to church. It is the very fiber of his being, and radiated from his whole personality. As I listened, I felt my heart glow in the warm radiance.

I can say of both Anna and Emmett Culligan what H.V. Morton wrote of the Irish he met in County Cork: "They lived in the shadow of God. They talked about Him as though He helped them that morning to bake the soda-bread in the peat-embers."

Emmett's faith showed most clearly when he talked about his beautiful daughter, married and the mother of a lovely family. God called her home when — according to human standards — she was most needed to take care of her young children. Mr. Culligan talked about his daughter as though she had simply stepped out of the room for a moment, and, before long, we would all be with her.

"How truly Christian," I thought to myself. "Here is a man who realizes that death is not the end of life, even for a second. Death is merely the passageway to greater life."

Emmett Culligan reached pinnacles of success in the business world that made him truly "a gentleman of distinction." He created an "empire" that circles the earth. With such an "empire" at his command, Emmett Culligan could have turned the proceeds to a life of luxury, and abandoned himself to the philosophy of pleasure proposed by the likes of Hugh Hefner. He could have followed the suntanned, charcoal-smoothed, V-8 voice of a contemporary, credit-card culture and spent his days sipping papaya juice in the shade of a palm tree on the island of Tahiti.

Instead, Emmett Culligan dedicated himself to the welfare of his fellowmen. Listen, now, as Emmet tells his own story:

"I have been in the marketplace fifty years, and have had much experience with Christ in business.

"During the first twenty-five years, I was a twentieth-century materialist. During that period my object was to make money and to share it with no one. Success, and the obtaining of money, was my aim. My muscles were continuously strained to the utmost. I never looked up or down. I read very little. I seldom rested. I was always going forward toward the vague success that modernists love to glorify. To be a millionaire has been a goal: I believed in this great American fallacy.

"In those days I never asked God's help. I never put my trust in His providence. I depended only on Culligan. While following this pattern of the materialistic world, I accomplished nothing of real value in twenty-five years. My confused thinking and false way of life fizzled out. I was a failure. I was tired, and I was discouraged.

"Then a great event happened in our family. Our seventh child was born — a giant thirteen-pound boy. He is now a priest. On the way home from the hospital after his birth, I stopped my second-hand Ford roadster alongside a cornfield.

"My six children had no groceries. There was no money in my pocket with which to buy them. It was in the depth of the 1930 depression.

"I got out of the little car, crawled through a barbed-wire fence, and pushed my way through a dozen rows of ripe corn stalks. I dropped to my knees, dug my hands into mother earth and shouted, 'God Almighty, I need help — I cannot go further myself. My little children need bread. I ask food, coal, and that our baby boy lives.'

"Although I am an Irish Catholic and have said daily prayers since childhood, this was the first time with full confidence in His providence that I begged sincerely for His help. Here is how my prayer in that cornfield was immediately and mysteriously answered. This message some way came through to me:

" 'Of course, I will help you and your family, Culligan. Why did you not come sooner? Have you not read . . . anything asked in my name will be granted? Now listen, Culligan — carefully. From this day forward, anything you ask for your family — anything — will be granted. But always on one condition. Anything I send you over and above that which is needed for your family you will not lock it up and hoard it, as is done on earth so often today.'

"From that day to this — for twenty-six years, I have taken God with me to the marketplace. I took a vow of poverty before leaving that cornfield.

"From that day forward He has been very generous. My prayer has been, 'Send us today our daily bread' — and this prayer ever since was always meant for my business associates as well as my family. He has not only sent daily bread but He sent it buttered.

"I have given away anything over and above that which was needed. I passed it along mostly to my fellow workers and also to my children, to give them a start of their own.

"They [the children] have rewarded us with forty-three grandchildren and one great grandchild. I have a little joke awaiting the usually stern tax collector when he opens my lockbox after my death. Because of the business I founded, which carries my name, I am considered to be 'loaded.' I deny this often, but few believe me. In a small bank box, to carry out this joke, there is one letter-size sheet of paper, and on this paper in my handwriting is written in large letters: 'Ha-ha, I sent it on ahead!'

"A short time after my meeting God in the cornfield, I had the nerve, in the depth of a serious depression, to start a new business.

"This time I wanted to take God with me to the marketplace. I started the Culligan soft-water industry in 1936 with only fifty dollars for permanent invested capital.

"Following God's providence, and His guidance, the business prospered. Because of my vow of poverty, and my desire to share with my fellow workers, a truly great prosperity and fellowship came to all of us. We came to 'love one another' as He commanded."

One of the most delightful memories I cherish of my visit with Anna and Emmett Culligan is that of the evening Rosary, which we said while sitting in lawn chairs on the terrace of their lawn overlooking the city of San Bernardino.

The sun had gone down in a symphony of color behind the western hills. Night was approaching on soft and beautiful feet, coming first gently and slowly from afar, then swiftly, and with her mantle of silence and darkness covering all things.

It was an hour of magic. Softly the daylight hours gave way to velvet hues, as twilight ushered in the night. Softly and yielding, earth and sky merged into one soliloquy. The sharp sights, the hard sounds of day, became softened and subdued; everything was bathed in glimmering beauty; the heart was lifted to an enchanted world, before darkness hid the real world from sight.

Truly, this was an hour made for prayer. Perhaps here, indeed, was the secret of its enchantment, that all creation at this hour praised God, singing of his beauty and entreating his benediction for the night. At this time the heart kneels; and did all men with one accord bow their heads in prayer, the kingdom of God would without hindrance and without delay be established on earth.

As I sat in the semidarkness listening to Emmett Culligan leading the Rosary, I thought of the words of Alfred Lord Tennyson:

> More things are wrought by prayer
> Than this world dreams of. Wherefore let thy voice
> Rise like a fountain for me night and day.
> For what are men better than sheep and goats
> That nourish a blind life within the brain,

> If, knowing God, they lift not hands in
>   prayer
> Both for themselves and those who call
>   them friends?
> For so the whole round earth is every way
> Bound by gold chains about the feet of
>   God.

Suffering and disappointments have made Anna and Emmett only too well aware of "The heartache and the thousand natural shocks that flesh is heir to," as Shakespeare tells us in *Hamlet*.

Some two years after my visit, Emmett Culligan suffered a severe fall that made walking impossible, and confined him to a bed of excruciating pain for many long months. Despite the pain-filled days that taxed his strength and spirit, Mr. Culligan did not complain. Instead, he drew good from his experience. "Now," he said, "I have a greater understanding for all the poor people who must suffer in this world."

One of Mr. Culligan's last public talks was to a Serra International convocation in Helena, Montana. He said, "Having made the love of God and my neighbor the guiding principle of my life, I hold myself in constant readiness for the greatest of all adventures — that of passing from this world into the next world. I look forward to this flight with greater eagerness, I am sure, and with a more joyful anticipation than even Col. John Glenn could have experienced during the countdown prior to his first orbital flight."

The first gentleman we considered in this chapter was from the world of politics. The second one was a businessman who took Christ with him into the marketplace. Our third man is astronaut James B. Irwin, who blasted off into space and found God while walking on the surface of the moon.

Irwin was the eighth man to walk on the moon. He viewed his moon journey as such an overpowering religious experience that he felt compelled to tell others about it. He retired from the U.S. Air Force and NASA in 1972 and founded High Flight, an interdenominational evangelistic foundation headquartered in Colorado Springs, Colorado. On the speaking circuit, attesting to his faith, Irwin said that his moon visit constituted a "spiritual awakening" for him.

During the fall of 1973, astronaut James Irwin appeared in five Midwestern states. The theme of his meeting was "The Now God." Irwin began his meetings on October 15 in Waupun, Wisconsin, and concluded them in Kalamazoo, Michigan, on October 25.

In his talks Irwin described his twelve-day journey into space and his three-day stay on the moon's surface. He gave his personal testimony of how he met God on the moon and how this experience changed his life.

To me, one of the most exciting things of the Bicentennial Year was the talk that astronaut Irwin gave in Watertown, South Dakota. The man who left his footprints and offered his prayers on the moon, and the first American to explore the fabled Mountains of the Moon, told his eager audience, "No matter how far man removes himself from the earth, God is still in control."

Irwin said that the greatest consolation the astronauts had as the *Saturn V* rocket boosted them into space "was knowing that we had the prayers of men and women everywhere. God became closer and closer to us as we ventured deeper and deeper into space. I felt God's presence amid the grandeur of the moon."

Irwin showed the audience a fragment of the rare white moon rocks that he and his colleagues brought back despite the great odds against finding them. Irwin said that it was his conviction God was instrumental in leading the astronauts to them.

Irwin admitted that when he blasted off for the moon atop the *Saturn V* rocket on July 26, 1971, he thought he was "just going up to get rocks and take some pictures." But, he said, he underwent many changes — psychological and spiritual.

"When you are on the moon," said Irwin,

"and see the earth, it is all so magnificent, for the colors of the earth give a beauty that is beyond description. As we went from earth to the moon and far out in space, we could actually see the outlines of the continents on earth, and the seas. It is so beautiful, so colorful, that I had a feeling over and over again of the glory of God."

On January 7, 1977, James B. Irwin had to undergo heart surgery, involving a triple bypass operation. Under these conditions Irwin might well have screamed, "Oh, God! Why do you strike me down and confine me to a bed of suffering? Don't you realize that I gave up my job as an astronaut so that I could go forth to the whole world and tell people how I found you on the moon? Why do you make it impossible for me to continue my work for you?"

With utter resignation Irwin accepted this suffering as coming from the hand of God. He took this tragedy in stride with the same courage he faced suffering in 1961. At that time Irwin was giving flight lessons in a small plane when the student sent it into a flat spin.

In the crash, Irwin broke both legs and his jaw, lost some teeth and, for a time, some of his memory. He was told he'd never fly again. But he recovered. In 1966 he was selected as an astronaut. Colonel Irwin served as lunar module pilot for *Apollo 15*, which was the fourth moon-landing mission, and the first to visit and explore the southeast edge of the Mare Imbrium (Sea of Rains).

On January 25, 1977, James Irwin sent me the following letter:

> Your prayers and good wishes are aiding me in my recovery from heart surgery. Mary, the children, and I are grateful for your prayers and concern.
>
> Despite my physical limitations, God continues to bless the outreach of High Flight Foundation. It will be a few weeks before I will be involved in a speaking program again, but my colleagues, Bill Rittenhouse, Bill Pogue, and Al Worden, are involved in many opportunities to communicate High Flight's message.
>
> Later this spring I plan to visit Ireland and West Germany, and we are presently considering invitations to speak in Scandinavia and Russia.
>
> Thank you again for your expression of love and concern.
> With warm regards,
> James B. Irwin

On August 11, 1981, James Irwin came to Omaha, Nebraska, to speak to the Christian Businessmen's Committee. At the luncheon, which was held at Anthony's Restaurant, James Irwin said that he could best sum up his experiences in space by reciting the poem "High Flight."

This poem was written in 1941 by a gifted poet, John Gillespie Magee, a pilot who was killed in World War II. I obtained permission to use "High Flight" from Mrs. John G. Magee, Sr., through her son David B. Magee.

> Oh, I have slipped the surly bonds of
> earth
> And danced the skies on laughter-
> silvered wings.
> Sunward I've climbed, and joined the
> tumbling mirth
> Of sun-split clouds — and done a
> hundred things
> You have not dreamed of — wheeled and
> soared and swung
> High in the sunlit silence. Hov'ring
> there,
> I've chased the shouting wind along, and
> flung
> My eager craft through footless halls of
> air.
> Up, up the long, delirious, burning blue
> I've topped the windswept heights with
> easy grace
> Where never lark, or even eagle flew.
> And, while with silent, lifting mind I've
> trod
> The high untrespassed sanctity of space,

Put out my hand, and touched the face
of God.

Irwin said that he would like to change the last line of the poem so that it would read, "God reached down and touched us."

So far in this chapter we have witnessed examples of a politician, a businessman, and an astronaut. Now I'll conclude this chapter by recalling some of the highlights from the life of the most talented and gifted priest I have ever known, Father Daniel A. Lord, S.J.

As national director of the Sodality of Our Lady in the United States, Father Lord gave untold hundreds of talks from coast to coast. He was a popular speaker on university, college, and high-school platforms across the country. In addition to giving retreats and lectures, he was editor of *The Queen's Work* magazine, which he published in St. Louis, Missouri.

During the summer months, he conducted summer schools of Catholic Action from one end of the country to the other. In addition to all this, he found time to write 30 books for adults, 48 books for children, 300 pamphlets, 25 plays, 12 pageants, and 3 musicals.

I consider myself most fortunate to have been a student at St. Louis University during the years that Father Lord was giving many of his talks and lectures at the university. Moreover, I thrilled to the sweeping pageants he produced in St. Louis. His musical productions often had a cast of over one hundred people who sang and danced to the delightful melodies and lightsome words that came leaping from his imagination.

I was always amazed how many things Father Lord managed to crowd into a lifetime that was punctured with so many spikes of pain and suffering. Time and again he was taken to St. John's Hospital where he would be confined from a few days to as long as five months.

No matter what the sufferings he encountered, Father Lord was buoyed up by two things. First and foremost was his deep faith in the joy in heaven to come. With enthusiasm Father Lord reechoed the words of St. Paul, ". . . the sufferings of this present time are not worth comparing with the glory that is to be revealed to us" (Romans 8:18).

"Life seems sweetest," remarked Father Lord, "when it melts gently into the Life that is our eternal promise."

In the years following my ordination, I had the unique good fortune of being allowed to cooperate with Father Lord in his work. I wrote a number of pamphlets for his publishing house, The Queen's Work, then located at 3115 South Grand Boulevard in St. Louis. Practically every month for fourteen years I had an article in his magazine, *The Queen's Work*.

It was during my contact with Father Lord

over the years I spent in St. Louis that I discovered the second greatest thing, next to his faith, that buoyed him up: It was his enthusiasm.

Father Lord had as his natural endowment and his cultivated ability what is undoubtedly the greatest of natural personal gifts. Beyond most men of this generation, he had enthusiasm. Everything in the world he found exciting. Everyone he met stimulated and roused his interest.

Father Lord was always finding new causes to espouse, new ideals to trumpet, new characters in history to grow ecstatic about, new truths that the world must hear. The past he found romantic; the present he found unendingly delightful; the future he saw through the rosy haze of optimistic hope.

I watched Father Lord stand before audiences and find so much delight in the subject he was handling that his infectious joy went right down into the hearts of his listeners.

He was always looking for the surprise that lies in everything and everybody. The more different, the more delightful. The more matter-of-fact, the more likely to be romantic.

Brilliant as was Father Lord's gift of writing, varied as were the mediums of his expression, all these powers faded into second place beside the one gift that made him the exultant, tireless, completely charming, vital personality — his boundless enthusiasm.

Father Lord wrote oftentimes to express the joy and delight, the surprise and amazement, the high discoveries and lofty adventures, the passionate dislikes and the gentle but gusty ironies, that kept his mind in constant vibration.

Father Lord's personal enthusiasms were what made life for him so zestful. They kept him eternally young. They made him the man one never forgot. They kept him alive, alert, the man of unlimited interests, of constantly widening vistas, of friends beyond counting and of knowledge wide, varied, and deep.

I am personally grateful to Father Lord for the delight I have found in his sparkle and wit and in the clear beauty of his prose and music. But beyond all else, I am grateful that he had the courage in a weary, tired, blasé age to find life zestful, and to live on the constant crest of enthusiasms.

Father Lord found the whole world a place of magic and mystery and surprises and delights, of glorious revelations of man's wonderful nature, of astounding glimpses of the glory of the world's Creator.

His zest for living brought him to the source of the fountain of life, Christ Jesus; and his enthusiasm for this world brought him to the feet of God.

How happy is the person who lives with eyes open to the wonders about us, and with ears attuned to earth's endless melodies! How happy the person who moves through earth's incredible fairyland, finding miracles at each turn of the road!

"To make a success of life," said Father Lord, "you've got to have deep enthusiasms and a wonder about the whole world you're looking at."

I had the golden opportunity of watching Father Lord move from enthusiasm to enthusiasm, his life growing richer, his experiences more varied, his knowledge constantly deeper and clearer, his human sympathies more enveloping, his own soul a thing of endless lights and fires!

To the students of St. Louis University Father Lord said, "If you would squeeze from each hour a new joy and from each friendship the full rich juice of comradeship and sympathetic understanding; if you would mature yet stay young, grow in years yet retain full resiliency — I give you the simple secret: Keep your enthusiasms. Develop your enthusiasms. Live enthusiastically."

In one of his talks to young people, Father Lord said, "The test of an educated person, whether he went to school or not, is simple: What does he do when someone else is not entertaining him?

"When he suddenly finds himself with a few hours of leisure, does he say delightedly, 'Now's the chance to do those interesting things I haven't had the chance to do' or 'Gosh, what am I going to do with all this time on my hands?' "

Father Lord was a man who practiced what he preached. A year and a half before his ordination, Dan Lord was stricken with a pronounced case of tuberculosis. When he checked in at St. John's Hospital in St. Louis, his weight had fallen from one hundred seventy-five to one hundred forty-five pounds. His bony frame was wracked with a persistent cough. The doctors insisted on a three-month rest cure.

On a cold and wintry day in February, Dan came to the infirmary of St. Stanislaus Seminary at Florissant, Missouri. For the next three months his kingdom was his room. He was alone almost the entire day.

The first thing he did was to read his way through the wonderful novels of Charles Dickens. His absorption was such that he forgot about the melting snows of early Florissant spring. He was living in the England of his fancy. With complete truth Dan Lord could apply to himself the words of the poet Everett Wentworth Hill:

> Within the confines of my room I may
> travel in my dreams

Roads of knowledge and of conquest —
all the world is mine, it seems.
Books, relating life's adventures into
places all unknown,
Carry me across the waters where my
thoughts have often flown.
So I sit at home and travel, far away to
some strange land,
Never lonesome in the knowledge which I
have at my command.

In the latter years of his life when Father Lord was confined as a patient to a hospital bed at St. John's, he refused to let this fact restrict his horizons. He believed that a shut-in's world may be as narrow as the bed on which he lies and the chair in which he sits; or his world may be as wide as infinity itself, if he will only look through his "mind's eye." It all depends on him.

"To make a success of life," said Father Lord, "you've got to have deep enthusiasms, and a wonder about the whole world. God help and pity the dull, unenthusiastic person."

Father Lord believed that the worst bankrupt in the world is the person who has lost enthusiasm. Let a person lose everything else but his enthusiasm, and he will come through again to success.

CHAPTER EIGHT

The Magic of Enthusiasm

In the preceding chapter I delved into the lives of several men I consider good examples of individuals who have discovered the magic of enthusiasm. In the same vein, I believe that the women discussed in Chapter 6 are individuals who, through a combination of positive attributes, including patience, perseverance, and enthusiasm, are individuals we can look to for inspiration in living life to the full.

With this in mind, let us see what "the magic of enthusiasm" is all about. The word "enthusiasm" comes from the Greek word *entheos*, which means "to be inspired by God" or "full of God."

Studies show that a person may have an IQ of only 95 or 100, but with a positive, optimistic, and cooperative attitude he can win more respect, earn more money, and achieve more success than his negative, pessimistic, and uncooperative counterparts with an IQ of

120 or more. Enthusiasm makes the difference.

Enthusiasm releases ambition that helps carry us over hurdles we might otherwise never leap. It endows the ups and downs of daily life with comeback strength, and keeps us going when the going is tough.

"None are so old," said Thoreau, "as those who have outlived enthusiasm." According to Norman Vincent Peale, enthusiasm has the power "to invest the prosaic, if not with romance, perhaps at least with exciting interest and meaning."

Ralph Waldo Emerson, who was an enthusiastic person himself, said, "Every great and commanding moment in the annals of the world is the triumph of some enthusiasm."

The outstanding characteristic of a little child is his enthusiasm. He thinks the world is terrific. He loves it. Everything fascinates him. The secret of a happy life is to carry the spirit of the child right into old age. And this means never losing enthusiasm.

Happiness and contentment in life depend more upon interest than assets.

In 1945, a journalist who was interviewing General Douglas MacArthur at his Tokyo headquarters was impressed by a framed poem on the general's desk. The poem, or essay, was called "Youth." The author apparently was anonymous. The general said this essay had been sent to him years before; he found it so inspiring he took it wherever he went. Because of General MacArthur's fondness for this essay, it often appeared in print and was called "General MacArthur's Credo."

Over twenty years later it was discovered that this essay was written many long years ago by Samuel Ullman. His message is as vital and necessary today as it was when the essay was written:

> Youth is not a time of life; it is a state of mind; it is not a matter of rosy cheeks, red lips, and supple knees; it is a matter of the will, a quality of the imagination, a vigor of the emotions; it is the freshness of the deep springs of life.
>
> Youth means a temperamental predominance of courage over timidity, of the appetite for adventure over the love of ease. This often exists in a man of sixty more than a boy of twenty. Nobody grows old merely by living a number of years. We grow old by deserting our ideals.
>
> Years may wrinkle the skin, but to give up enthusiasm wrinkles the soul. Worry, fear, self-doubt bows the heart and turns the spirit back to dust.
>
> Whether sixty or sixteen, there is in every human being's heart the lure of

wonder, the unfailing childlike curiosity of what's next and the joy of the game of living. In the center of your heart and mine there is a wireless station; so long as it receives messages of beauty, hope, cheer, and courage, you are young.

When the aerials are down, and your spirit is covered with the snows of cynicism and the ice of pessimism, then you have grown old, even at twenty. But so long as your aerials are up, to catch the optimism, there is hope you may die young at eighty.

Toward the end of her life, Helen Keller said, "Our worst foes are not belligerent circumstances, but wavering spirits." Again and again throughout her life, Helen Keller stated that "the best and most beautiful things in the world cannot be seen, or even touched. They must be felt with the heart."

It is said of Louis Pasteur that he had nothing to work with but the germ of an idea. But look where enthusiasm for that germ took him! You will never have an exciting world on the outside unless you have an exciting world on the inside.

One noon when Samuel Johnson was dining with friends in the Old Cheshire Cheese restaurant in London, the conversation got around to the benefits of a positive mental attitude.

Thumping the table with his fist for emphasis, Johnson said in a loud voice, "Egad, it's worth at least one thousand pounds a year to have a bright point of view."

According to Arthur Gordon in his book *A Touch of Wonder*, no other single human characteristic (with the possible exception of kindness) contributes so much to happy and successful living as does enthusiasm.

If you are enthusiastic, you have the capacity for generating excitement about ideas, people, events — anything! You respond to the stimuli of life not only with your five senses, and your brain, but with your emotions as well. You care, and in proportion as you care, you are alive — just as when you stop caring altogether, you are dead.

Enthusiasm is more than simple excitement, though it also involves affection for the object that arouses it. The enthusiastic person loves the thing he feels excited about. When he feels enthusiasm, he gives out love.

Because enthusiasm has optimism in it, because it's closely allied to cheerfulness, enthusiasm has the power to lift people over rough places in life. "Enthusiasm is a wonderful word," remarked Samuel Goldwyn, famous Hollywood producer, "but more — it is a wonderful feeling. It is a way of life."

Speaking of Hollywood, what would you think of a man who spent fourteen years as a cowboy, nine years as a farmer, and then turned into an "angel"?

Michael Landon did all this. For fourteen years (1959-73) he played a cowboy in *Bonanza*. For nine seasons (1974-83) he played a farmer in *Little House on the Prairie*. At seven o'clock on Wednesday evening, September 19, 1984, he began a new TV series called *Highway to Heaven*.

Michael says that the angel he portrays is not one who walks through walls, nor does he write magic notes. "He's just a person who has a job and a boss. I tried to make him as much like the rest of us as I possibly could. We are just trying to create an interaction between people."

Highway to Heaven won instant and wide acclaim for its inspiring message. This message is summed up by Michael in these words: "We are going to show that there are good people in this world. That if some people would try a little harder, people would realize that someone did care for them, and then maybe they would care a little bit more about themselves and their loved ones.

"I just want to make a show that I enjoy making, that my kids are going to like to watch and that people who feel like I do like to watch. We have to have some kind of role-models for kids and adults. For an awful lot of people, their only friends are on TV. I think it would be nice to show them that there are nice people in this world; to find ways to get [some people] out of the closets they live in."

Throughout all the many years of his TV series, Landon has believed all along that "you can change people by being nice to them."

Being nice to others and being enthusiastic go hand in hand. Enthusiasm is a magic spark that transforms "being" into "living." It makes hard work easy . . . and enjoyable. There is no better tonic for depression, no greater elixir for whatever happens to be wrong at the moment, than enthusiasm.

No person who is enthusiastic about his work has anything to fear from life. Opportunities are waiting to be grasped by the people who are in love with what they are doing.

My mother brought enthusiasm into the lives of her children. She had the ability to see romance and glory in everything. She loved the world, its beauty, and its people. She taught her children to deliberately look at the best side, to expect the good, the positive, the beautiful, in life.

By her life Mother proved that those who give free rein to their enthusiasm will never run short of it, for by so doing they are constantly adding to the supply. Mother retained her sense of wonder, and discovery. Time and again when Mother talked with friends and neighbors about their particular interests, they would almost glow incandescent as Mother's enthusiasm flowed into them.

The great philosopher Marcus Aurelius once said, "Our life is what our thoughts make it." What he means in plain words is that our thoughts rule, regulate, and decide the kind of life we will lead. Thus, our thoughts also determine what we will be.

The interesting thing is that your mental attitude toward yourself will reflect in your posture, the way you wear your clothes, your facial expressions, and your conversation. No wonder that Dorothy Canfield said, "We don't inherit our expressions; they are the signature of the years." And Joan L. Huegel says, "More than the clothes in your wardrobe, or even the way you do your hair . . . your most important fashion accessory is the expression that you wear."

"As a man thinketh — so is he!" You tell on yourself by the friends you see, by the very manner in which you speak, by the way you employ your leisure time, by the use you make of a dollar or dime.

James Allen would have us keep in mind: "As you think, you travel; as you love, you attract. You are today where your thoughts have brought you; you will be tomorrow where your thoughts take you. You will always gravitate toward that which you secretly most love. In your hands will be placed the exact results of your thoughts."

From the shadow-measuring Greek scientists to antibiotics, cyclotrons, and satellites, the world of science has seen a fabulous advance. Yet the loftiest experiments of all, according to Alexander Eliot, remain those of people. "Each man who lives is an experiment, self-controlled. He is both crucible and chemist in himself. Let him but open his own heart and mind, and the cosmos pours in upon him."

The world we look out upon through our eyes is — to a certain extent — the world we have created through our thinking in our moment of solitude.

Mark Twain in his autobiography reminds us: "Life does not consist mainly — or even largely — of facts and happenings. It consists mainly of the storm of thoughts that is forever blowing through one's head."

Marcus Aurelius centuries before put the idea this way: "A man's life is dyed the color of his imagination."

Helen Keller exhorted us: "Carry a vision of heaven in your hearts, and you shall make your home, your school, your world, correspond to that vision."

The great enduring realities are love and service. Joy is the holy fire that keeps our purpose warm and our intelligence aglow.

"Love, hope, faith, and trust — the unseen things that people feel," says Joyce A. Gordon, "are greater than the touching things that they collect and call them real."

Be a spendthrift in love! Love is the one treasure that multiplies by division: It is the one gift that grows bigger the more you take from it. It is the one business in which it pays to be an absolute spendthrift; give it away, throw it away, splash it over, empty your pockets, shake the basket, turn the glass upside down, and tomorrow you will have more than ever.

Live expectantly. Watch for the turns in the road that suddenly open new vistas of beauty before you.

Harleigh M. Rosenberger urges us to "make every day an adventure! The attitude with which you approach each day is important. Look at each day as though it were yours to enjoy for the first time in life."

Swiss psychologist Paul Tournier says, "There's a refreshing newness in seeing things through the eyes of a child." In his book *The Adventure of Living*, he urges parents to take their child by the hand and enter his world of adventure, perhaps to watch birds build a nest, or study a colony of ants making mounds of earth on the lawn.

I like to spend as much of Christmas Day as possible in the company of children. With children, everything takes on a kind of magic, the kind that produces an exciting afterglow.

On the occasion of the celebration of his eighty-ninth birthday, Herbert Hoover said, "The older I grow, the more I appreciate children. Children are the most wholesome part of the race, the sweetest, for they are freshest from the hand of God. Whimsical, ingenious, mischievous, they fill the world with joy and good humor. We envy them the freshness of adventure and discovery of life. In all these ways, children add to the wonder of being alive. In all these ways, they help to keep us young."

Ruth H. Underhill said, "Follow a child and you will find yourself at the very gateway of love, joy, and sincerity." Charles Dickens tells us, "I love little children, and it is not a slight thing when they, who are fresh from God, love us." No wonder that Elizabeth Barrett Browning wrote, "A child's kiss set on thy lips shall make thee glad."

An unknown author penned the following words under the title "To a Child":

"The spirit of wonder and adventure, the token of immortality, is given you as a child.

"May you keep it forever, with that in your heart which always seeks the gold beyond the rainbow, the meadows beyond the desert, the dawn beyond the sea, the growth of trees and the return of harvests, and the greatness of heroes.

"Keep your heart hungry for new knowledge; and keep your power of imagination."

According to the poet Grace Crowell: "Who looks at beauty with glad eyes is praising God all unaware."

One summer a number of years ago, Clare Boothe Luce went to Bermuda and did some skin diving. With a tank of air harnessed to her back, a rubber breathing tube in her mouth, a mask over her face, and with large rubber flippers on her feet, she swam down into the depths of the Atlantic.

Flippering and floating about in the watery jungles of the coral reefs, she was enthralled by all she saw. She wondered at the weird forms of the coral heads and branches and the exotic jewel-scaled fish that inhabit them. She saw diamond-drifting lights on the pearl-sand floors. She marveled at sea ferns dancing endlessly the lovely ballet of the underwater world.

When Clare returned to the sun-beaten deck of the boat, she felt like Alice returned through the looking glass. Forty feet below in the sea her spirit had become forty years younger. Joyful wonder had made her heart a child's again.

Then Clare asked herself: When was the last time she had so rejoiced at what she had seen?

The answer? When she was a child! Then,

everything in the world about her had seemed just as surprising and fascinating as what she had just seen. Suddenly she remembered the mornings and nights when, with wide, eager eyes, she had looked out the window of her bedroom.

There was so much that was miraculous then: the exquisite patterns of frost forming on the window pane; the great moon's cold winter cheek poking around the organdy cloud-curtains; an army of stars marching up the dome of heaven — white, and topaz, and misty red.

Clare said that she was grateful to the sea depths for reminding her that there is nothing on land or in the sea — a rose or rose coral, a star or starfish, a flight of birds, a school of fish, a pebble or a pearl — which is not a miraculous mirror of the whole universe.

"There is inspiration to be found on every hand," said Clare Boothe Luce, "if only we will permit ourselves to behold it in that silent and innocent wonder which is reverence's other name."

Did you ever stop to reflect that it may be your enthusiasm, or lack of enthusiasm, for a place that may determine whether you call it lovely or lonesome? It has been said that loneliness is not so much a function of place, as it is an attitude toward it.

According to Harry Paige, the idea of the

desert as a lonesome wasteland comes from white Easterners who remembered the greener hills of Vermont or New Hampshire.

The Navajo Indians who live in Arizona's Monument Valley and Canyon de Chelly do not consider the vast stretches of sand and rock as a lonely place. To them it brims with life and beauty. They accept without complaint or question the vagaries of the weather and the harshness of the elements as manifestations of the Power that governs the universe. Basic and uncomplicated people of the earth, they sing: "Beauty is before me . . . Beauty is behind me . . . Beauty is above me . . . Beauty is all about me."

According to Hugh Lavery, man is born to wonder. Everything important begins with wonder. Every child wonders, and feeds on surprise. Both the artist and the writer are aware that they do not know where their best insights come from. The real artistic gift is the gift of wonder. The persistence of a sense of the sacred at all times keeps wonder alive.

Wilfrid A. Peterson would have us keep in mind that the art of awareness is the art of learning how to awaken to the eternal miracle of life with its limitless possibilities. It is searching for beauty everywhere — in a flower, a mountain, a machine, a sonnet, a symphony.

It is keeping mentally alert to all that goes on around you; it is being curious, observant, imaginative, so that you may build an ever-increasing fund of knowledge of the universe.

God grant you know the loveliness that lies in common things. The smell of earth and summer rain. The brilliant flash of bluebirds' wings. The white-cloud frigates sailing high across the ocean of the sky. The laughter of a happy child. The velvet mystery of night. The daily miracle of light.

An inspired, unknown writer informs us that we will never enjoy the universe properly until the universe itself flows in our veins, until we are clothed with the heavens, and crowned with the stars — and until we perceive ourselves to be heirs of the whole world. Until we can sing and rejoice and delight in God, we will never truly enjoy the world.

No wonder Ralph Waldo Emerson tells us, "Never lose an opportunity of seeing anything that is beautiful, for beauty is God's handwriting — a wayside sacrament. Welcome it in every fair face, in every fair sky, in every flower, and thank God for it as a cup of blessing."

Let us keep in mind the beautiful words written centuries ago by Fra Angelico Giovanni, "The gloom of the world is but a shadow, behind it, yet within reach is joy. There is a radiance and glory in the darkness, could we but see, and to see, we have only to look. I beseech you to look!

"Life is so generous a giver, but we, judging its gifts by their covering, cast them away as ugly, or heavy, or hard. Remove the covering, and you will find beneath it a living splendor woven of love, by wisdom, with power.

"Welcome it, grasp it, and you touch the angel's hand that brings it to you. Everything we call a trial, a sorrow, or a duty, believe me, that angel's hand is there; the gift is there, and the wonder of an overshadowing presence. Our joys too; be not content with them as joys. They too conceal diviner gifts.

"And so at this time I greet you. Not quite as the world sends greetings, but with profound esteem, and with the prayer that for you, now and forever, the day breaks and the shadows flee away."

There is no need to go to the far corners of the earth in search of heroic souls who have surrendered themselves to God. In the circle of your friends you can without doubt find many who could tell a thrilling romance of their soul's surrender to God's love and will.

The inspiration of their lives will continue long after God has called such generous souls home. Like a great masterpiece of music, or inspiring picture, the lives of such people echo a theme that is consoling, encouraging, a thing of beauty and a joy forever. They give proof to the words of the poet, "God's in His Heaven, all's right with the world."

CHAPTER NINE

New Horizons

The space age began on October 4, 1957, when the Soviet Union put *Sputnik I,* the first man-made satellite, into orbit. On January 31, 1958, *Explorer I,* America's first satellite, was put into orbit. Although *Explorer I* weighed only thirty-one pounds, this tiny moonlet announced to the world that America had entered the space age.

On February 20, 1962, Lieutenant Colonel John H. Glenn, Jr., became the first American to orbit the earth. He made three orbits around the earth in just under five hours. He splashed down in his spacecraft, *Friendship 7,* in the Atlantic.

Christmas week of 1968 was unique. For the first time in the history of the world, three American astronauts blasted off planet earth atop a *Saturn V* rocket to cruise out and circle the moon. The Wise Men of old rode camels across a desert of shifting sand, while their modern counterparts rode a space capsule across a desert of empty space.

On Christmas Eve, as the *Apollo 8* capsule orbited around the moon, the crew panned their TV cameras across the vast naked plains, barren mountains, and huge craters seventy miles beneath them.

As the bleak and desolate lunar scene continued to pass slowly beneath *Apollo 8*'s windows, William Anders's soft voice was heard, "For all the people back on earth, the crew of *Apollo 8* has a message that we would like to send to you: 'In the beginning, God created the heaven and earth.' "

Each of the three *Apollo 8* astronauts took part in reading the first ten verses from the Bible. After the Scripture reading, Commander Frank Borman added, "And from the crew of *Apollo 8*, we close with good night; good luck, and a Merry Christmas and God bless all of you — all of you on the good earth."

Over half a year later, on Sunday, July 20, 1969, astronauts Neil A. Armstrong and Edwin E. Aldrin, Jr., descended to the surface of the moon in the *Apollo 11* lunar module *Eagle*. As Neil Armstrong stepped onto the moon's dusty surface, a message was radioed to millions of anxiously waiting people on earth: "That's one small step for a man, one giant leap for mankind."

I have always been impressed by the fact

that during the years that our astronauts were blasting off for new horizons in space, equally new horizons were being opened up in our religion.

Listen, now, to the words of Father Martin D'Arcy, S.J., internationally famous lecturer and author: "We have reached a moment in history as critical as when Constantine the Great confessed himself a Christian. We are living in a moment more important than that of the barbarian invasion, or even the Reformation. The last few years have brought an extraordinary change in the whole atmosphere of religion." According to Father D'Arcy, the thrilling thing today is the "rediscovery" of the joy of Christianity and the true meaning of Easter.

Father Daniel J. O'Hanlon, S.J., professor of theology at Alma College, has some thoughts he would like to share with us:

"Modern scholarship shows more and more clearly that the . . . writings which contain the essence of Christianity in its purest and richest form, the books of the New Testament, were all composed under the impact of the Resurrection.

"That was when the Resurrection was, in practice as well as in theory, the central Christian reality.

"It was the overpowering reality of the risen Lord which drove Paul to the ends of the earth, and produced those letters in which

---

language breaks down, unable to capture this joyous mystery in mere words. The author of the Fourth Gospel is so absorbed in the victory of Christ over death that the Passion is almost neglected.

"This focus on the Resurrection does not stop with the books of the New Testament. The preaching of Christ in the early Church was all Resurrection-centered.

"Christian art in its earliest beginnings, and for many centuries afterward, reveals this centrality of the Resurrection.

"The martyrs saw their death in union with Christ as the gateway to victorious resurrection with Him.

"Read the liturgies of the early Church. They all show us that when Christians came together to worship, the risen Lord was at the center of it all."

Here now Father O'Hanlon brings out a beautiful truth, so inspiring and encouraging, it should be shouted from the housetops:

"The Eucharist, too, was celebrated in the radiance of the Resurrection. It was in a spirit of joy that Christians assembled for the community banquet of thanksgiving and praise, realizing that He to whose sacrifice they were united was the victorious, risen Christ now reigning in glory.

"Realistic representations of the crucifixion were unknown until the fifth century, and in

Western Europe it was not until the end of the 13th century that emphasis in representation of the crucifixion turned from the triumph of Christ to His sufferings.

"In the centuries which followed, the human suffering of Christ and His Mother was emphasized more and more. We move into the era of swooning madonnas and gory crucifixes.

"There was much melancholy piety in the period that culminated in the Reformation. Perhaps it was the widespread feeling of collective discouragement, the loss of joy and triumph which accompany the risen Christ that made the tragedy of the 16th century possible."

Today, thank God, we are returning to the view of the early Church. As Father O'Hanlon reminds us, "Christ is not weak now; Christ is the Christ who has won the victory over death and reigns in power. Weakness is only a passing phase; power and victory are the permanent reality.

"Easter was the original Christian feast, a purely Christian product. This is just what we would expect, since the heralds of the gospel preached, first, the risen Lord reigning in power.

"The mystery of Easter is a thing of dynamic fulfillment. Easter means that the central reality is not death, but life."

In concluding, Father O'Hanlon reminds us

that we should learn and teach *a genuinely resurrection-centered theology.*

When I was in the ancient city of Rome, I walked down beneath the city into the dimly lit tunnels that are the catacombs, and "discovered" one of the truths mentioned by Father O'Hanlon.

Countless other people before me who visited the catacombs made the same "discovery" no doubt, but no one I know has phrased it as well as H.V. Morton in his fascinating book *A Traveller in Rome.*

"One feature of the catacombs lingered in my mind," says Mr. Morton. "In all the hundreds of miles of tunnels not once is Christ pictured on the Cross. The Christ of the catacombs is a youthful, beardless figure in Greek dress, who, at first glance, might be Apollo or Orpheus."

The main impression one absorbs from a trip through the catacombs is expressed by Mr. Morton: "The atmosphere [of the catacombs] is one of faith and trust. The epitaphs carved on the tombs are happy and confident.

"The message they give is one of faith, hope, and charity. One echoes the words of a medieval pilgrim who wrote on the walls: 'There is light in this darkness: there is music in these tombs.' "

"It is wonderful," said Father Al Thomas, in his syndicated column in Catholic newspapers, "that the Church is turning back to the mystery of Christ's Resurrection as the central miracle of His life. Only in the last few years has a 15th station — the Resurrection — been added to the Way of the Cross.

"The emphasis once placed on the wounds of Christ and the burden of our sins which He took upon Himself is now yielding to the glorified body of Christ, and the similar radiance and brilliance awaiting us in the future life."

The resurrection of Christ is the foundation of our Christian hope — and not just because he died and rose again, but because the risen Lord lives right now. He lives as you and I live, only he lives much more fully. In his risen life, right now, Christ exists not for his own sake — he lives for you and me.

This fact is our absolute guarantee that we as human beings will be fulfilled. We will come to full happiness, full in this life as much as this life can permit and full in the life which lies beyond. The context of Christianity is one of love; it is one of thanksgiving; it is one of profound quiet, peaceful happiness.

It is interesting to note that at one time the Church year began with Easter, the feast around which all our liturgical worship revolves. For three centuries it was the only one to be celebrated throughout the Church. It corresponds to the Jewish Pasch, or Passover, and the transition from the Jewish Pasch to the Christian Easter was made by Christ himself.

The "Blessings of the Fire and the Candle" show that the paschal supper used to be held on the night of the full moon, the brightest night of the month. The commemoration of our Lord's resurrection makes Holy Saturday night the brightest night in the Church year. And the triumphal proclamation of the Exsultet picks up all paschal echoes from Sinai to the Last Supper. "This is the night in which Christ rose victorious from the grave. O truly blessed night."

Esther Baldwin York tells us: "The event of the Resurrection brought a new perspective to the vision of man. No longer was he restricted to the little distance of an earthly existence. The horizon melted away, as it were, and he could glimpse beyond the clouds the golden glory of eternal life."

"Because of the Resurrection," said Father Ellwood Kieser, "the entire human situation is alive with the divine presence. The human is now permeated with the divine. God is not far away. He is as close as the closest human being. He is closer to us than we are to ourselves. He has made Himself one with our humanity."

No wonder St. Paul exclaimed, "Death is swallowed up in victory. . . . O death, where is thy sting?" (1 Corinthians 15:54-55).

Since the Church is now placing emphasis

---

on "resurrectional theology" — looking ahead to the great joys in heaven to come — it is not surprising to find the beautiful new cathedral in Lincoln, Nebraska, called the "Cathedral of the Risen Christ."

The brochure issued at the time of the dedication of the Cathedral of the Risen Christ reminds us, "The Resurrection of the First Easter is the central thought and mystery of Christianity. It is the heart of our faith and our hope. And so it is the theme of the new Cathedral. All things in the Cathedral of the Risen Christ tell of this truly tremendous event. The windows, the art work, the statuary announce as did the angel on Easter: 'He has risen even as He said. Alleluia!' "

"We are Easter people and Alleluia is our song" are the words of St. Augustine. These words are not just a happy turn of phrase from an ancient Easter sermon. To call Christians Easter people, Alleluia people, is to describe the very heart of Christian faith.

The greatest feast of the year is not only a celebration of God's powerful love. It is also a celebration of our power in the risen Lord. We live our lives shot through with Easter faith.

The late Father John Reedy, C.S.C., would have us keep in mind that our ultimate optimism and joy grow out of the beliefs we profess. We don't foolishly blind ourselves to the reality of suffering and pain. Our experience of pain and suffering, however, is tempered by the conviction that we can confidently entrust the outcome to God.

According to Juan Arias, "Easter ought to be simply the day on which, in a very special way, we Christians cry out to each other, and especially the day when, all together, we cry out to the world the joy of our certainty of resurrection, the ecstasy of our new love, our hope of the final triumph of life over death."

In words that vibrate like bugle notes, Father John Powell, S.J., informs us: "By all means join the dance and sing the songs of a full life. You are on your way to an eternal home which is prepared for you. Remember that the sufferings of this present stage of your life are nothing compared to the glory that you will see revealed in you someday.

"On your way to our eternal home, enjoy the journey. Let your happiness be double, in the joyful possession of what you have and in the eager anticipation of what will be.

"Say a resounding 'Yes!' to life and to love. Someday you will come up into my mountain, and then for you all the clocks and calendars will have finished their counting. Together with all my children, you will be mine, and I will be yours forever."

Our belief in the risen Christ does not eliminate all problems, pain, and anxiety. The suffering and difficulties of good people constitute one of the most persistent challenges to our belief in a God who looks on his people, each one of us, with gracious love.

With masterful skill, Father John Reedy informs us, "Our thoughts run something like this: If I were God, if I were Master of the Universe and lover of every man, woman, and child, cancer would not be part of the human experience; despots would never win control of nations; misunderstanding, hurts, and fears — between nations and between members of families — would be reconciled.

"If I were God . . . but I'm not.

"The fundamental gift which God offered to us in Jesus was not the relief from all pain. Instead, the Lord shared our weariness, our experience of misunderstanding, rejection, betrayal, pain, and death.

"In His resurrection on Easter morning, He gave us the sign, the assurance, that all the hurt, the disappointments, the suffering will finally culminate in the glory of the God who loves us."

In 1938, when I was teaching Sioux Indians at Holy Rosary Mission in Pine Ridge, South Dakota, one of my high-school students asked, "Why do we have Easter eggs?"

I answered his question by saying that the Easter egg is a symbol of the Resurrection, a sign of life to come, a reminder that the cold grave will one day burst with life and light.

We do not know exactly when the egg was first associated with Easter, but the symbol of the chick breaking forth from the egg and the emergence of life from the sepulcher has persisted through long ages. The coloring of the Easter eggs represents the dawning hues of the Easter sun. The color red is also used to symbolize the Easter joy.

The Slavic people used exquisite designs on eggs and each design had a special meaning. A flower, for example, represented charity and love; a stag or deer, good health.

In no place in the world has the art of decorating the Easter egg been more beautifully perfected than in the Ukraine, now a republic of the Soviet Union. A number of the Ukrainians who came to Canada still carry on the tradition of decorating eggs. In fact, the Ukrainians who live in Vegreville, Alberta, have erected as a symbol of their town a thirty-one-foot high aluminum "Easter egg" intricately decorated with vivid symbols.

It is interesting to note that in the early ages of the Church, the day on which a person died was considered his birthday — his birthday into glory, and joy, and happiness without end; hence it was not the custom to use black at funerals. In fact, we know that St. Cecilia and other famous martyrs were laid to sleep wearing regal cloth of gold.

"Why should you wear black garments of

mourning," asked St. Cyprian, "since those for whom you mourn have put on the shining garments of glory?" With the passage of centuries, however, black found its way into the vestments. Today, thank God, the new funeral rites have brought us back to the happy outlook of the early Church.

The funeral Mass is no longer called a "Requiem" Mass. It is called the Mass of the Resurrection, and the priest wears white vestments instead of black.

It was entirely fitting that the great, kindhearted Archbishop Paul Hallinan, who did so much to bring about the new liturgy, was the first to benefit from the new rite. When acute hepatitis took the fifty-six-year-old churchman's life, the U.S. apostolic delegate, Archbishop Luigi Raimundi, was the principal concelebrant of the Mass, which included white vestments, joyful Easter music, prayers and readings with a resurrection theme, and the presence of the paschal candle near the casket.

One of the great heroes of modern times is Dietrich Bonhoeffer, a young Lutheran pastor who was convinced that it was his duty as a Christian to work for Hitler's defeat.

In Germany he is glorified as one of the heroes of the resistance who preserved the honor of their nation by resisting Nazism. Bonhoeffer's former teacher and friend, Reinhold Niebuhr, said that Bonhoeffer's achievement as a martyr and exemplar belonged to "the modern Acts of the Apostles."

In February 1945, with the Russian armies inexorably closing in on Berlin from the east, Bonhoeffer was among the prisoners taken to Buchenwald. Payne Best, a British Intelligence officer incarcerated with Bonhoeffer and other prisoners, wrote in his book *The Venlo Incident* that "Bonhoeffer was all humility and sweetness; he always seemed to me to diffuse an atmosphere of happiness, of joy in every smallest event in life, and of deep gratitude for the mere fact that he was alive. He was one of the very few men I have met to whom his God was real and ever close to him."

Bonhoeffer and Best were among the prisoners who, on April 3, began the slow journey by truck southward to the extermination camp at Flossenburg.

On April 8, a Sunday, the prisoners asked Bonhoeffer to conduct a meditation on the Bible verses for the day. "He had hardly finished his last prayer," Best recalled, "when two evil-looking men in civilian clothes came in and said, 'Prisoner Bonhoeffer, get ready to come with us.'

"These words had come to mean one thing only. We bade him good-bye — he drew me aside — 'This,' he said, 'is for me the beginning of life.' "

Father Charles Gallagher, S.J., would have

us keep in mind that the corollary to Jesus' being risen is that we ourselves are one day to experience the same thing. We do not truly believe in Easter if we do not believe that resurrection will be ours and live accordingly.

"The Resurrection," says Father Gallagher, "should be a brilliant sun that lights our whole existence every day of our lives. Do we really have faith that one day we will rise again, that we will be able to touch each other, hug, hold hands, caress, talk, and listen to each other?"

According to Father Gallagher, we should "share with one another what that promise of Jesus means. Talk about the deceased members of the family. Share how we imagine them now and what we will say to them when we meet them again."

How wonderful to realize that we will enjoy our loved ones in heaven as we do now, as individuals. Becky will still be her charming, lovely self. Sid will be as vigorous as he was when he climbed the heights of the Blarney Castle to kiss the fabled stone.

In heaven your loved ones will have a personal love for you as warm and throbbing as when you held them in your arms. In heaven we shall love our dear ones in such an ecstasy of delight that our poor hearts could not survive the seraphic intensity without first sharing in the divine nature.

Recall the most perfect love you have ever

known among mortals: the tender love of a
young couple who stand before the altar and
give themselves into each other's keeping until
death silently breaks the bond; the mature,
golden love of this same couple when
anniversary bells ring in the fiftieth year of
their mutual devotion and constant love.

Whether it is the love of a mother for her
child, or a friend's love for a friend, or an uncle
for a niece or nephew, each and all of these loves
will grow a thousand times greater. Take this
love, multiply it a billion times a billion, and
still you have not a measure of the love of the
blessed in heaven.

Those you love now will be with you. The
wonderful human love that affords you
moments of charm to make memory a joy —
that love that comes as a star from heaven to
point the way, and lead us to its home — that
love will bloom and grow again.

The most exciting and magic three little
words in the world will form the theme of a
beautiful rhapsody. It will be played over and
over again in different tempos and with
exquisite colorings, but always its divine refrain
will return like a haunting melody, "I love you."

In the eloquent silence of the moment when
love is all a-tangle in your throat, and words are
too small for the long thoughts of love, you clasp
hands with your loved one and carry on a

conversation without talking. Heaven is love forevermore.

In that wonderful tomorrow, Christ our brother will take our hand in his. Our fingers shall fold upon the eternal power that guides the massive planets whirling down their orbits and draws from gleaming stars the light to glorify his name.

In words soft and low, and with ineffable tenderness, Christ will say, "I love you. I loved you so much that I came from heaven to earth and died for you. Now, I take you with me to dwell forever in happiness."

God loves his children immeasurably more than the most ardent human lover his beloved. The main joy of heaven is God himself, the source of all love, beauty, and happiness.

Men search for beauty and love because God puts that urge in their hearts. In heaven we shall possess the source of all beauty and love. The soul — thirsty for beauty, and hungry for love — realizes that the God of limitless beauty has loved it with an everlasting love, will love it with an everlasting love, and, what is more astounding, is pleased to be loved by this person in return.

The appreciation of beauty, which is judged to be a part of the faculty of love, expands and grows as it is nourished on what is beautiful.

Man can never be loved enough by his fellowman. Even between the closest of lovers there are times when thoughts and desires so mysterious and deep stir within the heart that they somehow defy and escape analysis of human expression.

In heaven our hearts will rest in God, in God whose grandeur and beauty we see reflected all around us. Blue waters whitened against a granite cliff, children's upturned faces holding wonder like a cup, music like a curve of gold, tulips waving in the breeze, silver shadows on a moonlit branch — all these are tiny images telling us of God's wondrous beauty and charm.

When the winds are breathing low and the rain-awakened flowers open dewy buds, you can almost sense the presence of God hovering about you with his power and might. G.K. Chesterton remarked, "Sunlight in a child's hair is like the kiss of Christ upon all the children."

It is God whose fingers scooped out the depths of the Grand Canyon. He pours the waters of the Mississippi down through the fertile valleys of the Midwest. He arches the great circle of the sky and tints it with dazzling colors.

God tapestries the mountains in wild flowers of exquisite design to rival the handiwork of proud and lovely ladies. Our God is a God of beauty, of joy and happiness.

CHAPTER TEN

Adventures Unlimited

"Hey, this is neat!" exclaimed the
astronaut as he twisted and turned in
the vastness of space, one hundred
sixty-five miles above Hawaii. It was February
7, 1984. Navy Captain Bruce McCandless II,
mission specialist on the space shuttle
Challenger's STS-41-B journey, became the first
human satellite by performing a feat no
astronaut in history had ever attempted: The
forty-six-year-old astronaut stepped into space
without being fastened to a line.

"This is beautiful . . . super . . . superb," he
radioed back to *Challenger* and mission
controllers at NASA in Houston, Texas, as he
maneuvered up to three hundred twenty feet
away from the orbiter. Then, referring to
astronaut Neil Armstrong — who made the now
famous statement "That's one small step for a
man, one giant leap for mankind," when he
landed on the moon in 1969 — McCandless said,
"That may have been one small step for Neil,
but it's a heck of a big leap for me."

One glorious day in your future, you will be able to surpass Bruce McCandless, without the need of his $100,000 space suit and special backpack called an MMU (manned maneuvering unit). That day will come when we shall have our own glorified body, similar to the body of Christ. The resurrection of Christ, in fact, is a "preview" of our own personal resurrection.

Today the Church is stressing "resurrectional theology" so that we may draw comfort and consolation from the realization that we will have our own personal resurrection. Our bodies will be like our Lord's.

Just what exactly will our glorified body be like? For the answer, go back to the first Easter Sunday afternoon when the apostles were gathered together in the upper room in Jerusalem. Every door and window was locked and bolted. Suddenly, mysteriously, graciously, Christ stood in their midst, his body having passed through the very walls of the room.

Our bodies will be made like unto Christ's. We shall be able to travel anywhere we wish. We shall not be hindered by walls, doors, or mountains; nor will our bodies be affected by material things. Suffering and pain will be things of the past.

Suppose that you had your glorified body now. If you wish to explore the giant planet Jupiter, all you would have to do is to make the wish, and there you will be. What a thrill it would be to stand on the King of the Planets. Jupiter is so large it could swallow thirteen hundred Earths. Its volume is one and a half times the volume of all the other planets put together. It has more than twice the mass or weight of all the other planets combined.

The most beautiful feature on Jupiter is likewise the most mysterious. It is the Great Red Spot. It was first seen by the Englishman Robert Hooke in 1680. The egg-shaped spot is some thirty thousand miles long and eight thousand miles wide. At times the spot becomes bright red. Sometimes it completely disappears. The spot appears to be something floating in the atmosphere. It looks like a raft or an island. The material inside the spot moves in a circle in six days. Over the centuries the spot itself has drifted around the planet.

Pioneers X and *XI* reported that the Great Red Spot may be a hurricanelike storm, that the colorful cloud bands are rising and falling air masses.

You could see for yourself one of the most delightful and beautiful surprises that was brought to us by *Voyager 1* in March 1979 — the discovery of the ring around Jupiter. The ring is about 35,000 miles above the tops of Jupiter's clouds. The ring appears to be some 4,000 miles wide and about 18 miles thick. The material in the ring may be made of broken rock and "ashes" thrown out into space by the volcano on

Io, one of Jupiter's moons. Or the material may have come from an ancient satellite that was torn apart by Jupiter's tremendous gravitational pull.

Instead of dashing out into space, you may wish to dive into the ocean's depths and examine for yourself some of the most startling deep-sea discoveries of modern times that were made possible by the mini-sub *Alvin*.

It was on April 21, 1979, when two scientists and a pilot folded themselves into the cramped interior of this small research submarine and slowly descended to a depth of nine thousand feet in the Pacific Ocean.

The sub's headlights illuminated a surreal landscape of lava plains and boulders, and finally, the object of their search — a hydrothermal vent where scalding water spewed from cracks and fissures. The milky-blue hot water streaming out of the cracks swirled around bouquets of tube worms that looked like giant red flowers on white stalks.

These giant tube worms stretched out to eight feet in length. Like turtles in their shells, the worms hid inside rubbery white tubes three inches in diameter, extending only a spongy red plume out of one end. The worms clustered around the vents, the bottoms of their tubes anchored to the rocks at the top of a fissure, their plumes waving gently in the flow.

In the cooler water farther from the vent

there were foot-long clams, pink fish, snails, shrimps, and sulphur-yellow mussels. Crabs scuttled in and out of the hot water to nip pieces from the worms' plumes.

The biological significance of these giant tube worms and other creatures is that this deep-sea life uses a source of energy other than the sun as a basis for their lives.

If you wish to explore sunken ships, you may wish to dive into two and a half miles of water some 560 miles off Newfoundland to examine the *Titanic*, the most luxurious liner of its time. The liner, 882 feet long, was thought to be unsinkable; but on its maiden voyage an iceberg buckled the 12-inch-thick plates on the hull enough to create a fatal leak. The mammoth steamer went down four hours after striking the iceberg on April 14, 1912, with the loss of some 1,500 lives. About 700 escaped via lifeboats.

Perhaps you may prefer to stand on North Cape, the northernmost point of Europe on August first and behold an amazing sight — sunrise follows sunset by one second. This is the land of the midnight sun. All during the month of July the sun remains above the horizon. On August first, for the first time in weeks, the bottom rim of the sun just touches the horizon at midnight. The next second the sun starts to climb back into the sky. It is sunrise.

One of the things you most certainly would

like to do if you had your glorified body now is to cruise out to Butte, Montana, and see the new ninety-foot statue of our Blessed Mother that stands on a mountaintop more than eighty-five hundred feet above sea level overlooking the city. This steel statue that towers over the East Ridge on the Continental Divide east of Butte is called Our Lady of the Rockies.

The idea for this statue began in 1979 when Bob O'Bill, a copper miner, promised our Blessed Mother that if his wife, Joyce, would recover from a serious illness, he would put up a small statue in Mary's honor.

What O'Bill had in mind was a five-foot statue placed in a Butte park, but two friends came up with the idea of a ninety-foot version. A group of people of all faiths formed a nonprofit foundation to raise money for construction of the statue and a site to place it on. The owner of the site agreed to a permanent lease at no cost.

Leroy Lee, a fifty-one-year-old ironworker, began work on the statue in 1981. With only a grade-school education and a journeyman's knowledge of mathematics behind him, he took on what would be the biggest job in his ironworking career.

He started with a ten-inch ceramic figure of Mary brought into the welding shop by Bob O'Bill. Using a twelve-inch ruler, Lee began thinking in terms of scale and plotting the structure on graph paper with the help of his wife, Pat, a schoolteacher.

He started the right hand in the summer of 1982, using scrap exhaust pipe from heavy trucks for the fingers. "If I can't build a hand, then I can't build a ninety-foot statue," he told himself. Once the hand was completed, Lee began work on the head. It seemed a nearly impossible task. "I took the iron and just heaved it in a pile," he said.

On the following Monday Lee intended to tell Joe Roberts, the owner of a local equipment yard, who provided space for the project, to find someone else to do it. He would tell Joe, "I'm no sculptor."

On Sunday morning Lee, a converted Catholic, went to Mass at St. Ann's. During the Mass Lee prayed to Mary: "If you want me to build you, show me how." That night, Lee said, it became clear to him how to plot the entire sculpture on a grid. "It just flowed," he said. Lee and a team of volunteers, including O'Bill, completed the sixty-ton structure in 1985.

On Saturday, February 25, 1984, I had a most unusual experience. I had the unique privilege of having dinner with the late Marlin Perkins, the star of TV's award-winning series *Wild Kingdom*.

As I listened to the inspiring story of his life and adventures with animals, I began to wish that I had my glorified body so that I too could travel to such exotic locales as West Africa, with its wild gorillas; the Kalahari Desert, where Marlin filmed the primitive bushmen; Central and South America, where he collected snakes, crocodiles, and pink dolphins; the Mount Everest region, where he and Sir Edmund Hillary searched for the legendary abominable snowman; Lapland, where he drove reindeer herds in a blizzard; and Australia's Great Barrier Reef, where he filmed dangerous sharks at close quarters.

In our delightful world to come, we shall have more than the thrill of our glorified bodies. Our minds will embrace all branches of truth. The mysteries of medicine, chemistry, and the physical universe will unfold before us.

One of the mysteries we look forward to solving is that of gravity. Gravity is most unusual. No substance we know of can shield us from gravity, make it weaker, or change the direction of its attraction. We cannot increase it or bend it.

By contrast, see what you can do with a beam of light. You can use a prism to bend a beam of light. A mirror will reflect it. A black cloth will absorb it.

You can send electricity through copper wires. Rubber and glass may be used as insulators to keep electricity where you want it.

Scientists point out that no one really knows for sure just what gravity is. In the latter part of his life, Einstein tried to show that gravity, electricity, and magnetism were all parts of one universal law, but he did not complete his work. Newton himself never claimed to have explained its nature, only its behavior.

Another mystery we can look forward to solving is that of the Ice Capades. The U.S. Air Force was so interested in them it conducted a "special investigation." Why is it that ice skaters can spin at high speeds without becoming dizzy? If the Air Force could find the answer, perhaps they could keep their pilots from becoming dizzy when they go into a spin.

The investigation carried out by the Air Force did not solve the mystery, but it did bring to light some interesting facts. When skaters spin, they do so in a counterclockwise motion, opposite to the motion of the hands of a clock. The skaters generally focus their gaze at a point in the ceiling. If they close their eyes, they become dizzy. And if they spin in the opposite direction, they become dizzy.

Another mystery we can look forward to solving is that of sight. Some people think that they see with their eyes, but this is not so. Our eyes are photoelectric cells that change light into electricity. The retina is a living tissue of about one hundred thirty million cells, sensitive to light. When light hits these cells — called rods and cones because of their shape — they go to work.

Cones work in daylight and give us color vision. Rods give us only black and white. Cones are most numerous at the fovea, a very small pit, or tiny spot, in the retina, where the eye gets its clearest images. The rods and cones are connected to the optic nerve. The optic nerve may be compared to a telegraph cable that gives the brain a private line to what is going on in our world.

Oddly enough, the brain itself never directly experiences the form of energy we call light. The brain rests in darkness inside your skull. The rods and cones change the energy of light into electrical signals that are sent along the optic nerve to the brain. When this electricity reaches your brain, your brain interprets, or translates, these electrical signals into what we call sight. Just how this is done is a mystery.

In the fall of 1943, I was in my third year of studying theology at St. Marys, Kansas. In October, Father Daniel A. Lord, S.J., came from St. Louis to give our annual retreat. He was by far the most inspiring retreat master I ever had. During those wonderful days from the first to the tenth of October, I made copious notes. These notes have become one of my most cherished possessions.

Father Lord reminded us that it is curiosity

that leads to discovery and invention. But it is much more than that. It is another promise of eternal happiness. It is an appetite that God gave us, and he means to satisfy it. God did not intend to let us die with only the tiniest point in the inexhaustible universe tentatively explored.

In heaven our curiosity will be stronger than ever. And we shall have unlimited opportunity and all eternity to satisfy it. We shall be faced with the glorious paradox, the exciting contradiction: Our curiosity will range out into infinity, always satisfied and always hungry.

Even here on earth we never grow weary of a really beautiful painting or a lovely face. Think what it will be in heaven, when we shall have God himself, the source of all beauty, before us.

It should give us a thrill to know that the curiosity we have is hardly more than an appetizer for the heaven that lies ahead. What we have learned in our brief and limited existence on this earth is but a glimmer of what we shall know in our home to come. On that wonderful day we shall be able to recapture from the past all that we missed. We shall be free from the chains of time and space.

Heaven is the place where human curiosity will be eternally stimulated, always satisfied, and never satiated.